THE FUCHSIA GROWER'S HANDBOOK

THE FUCHSIA GROWER'S HANDBOOK

Ron Ewart

BLANDFORD

Blandford Press
An imprint of Cassell
Artillery House, Artillery Row, London SW1P 1RT

First published 1989

Distributed in the United States by
Sterling Publishing Co, Inc,
2 Park Avenue, New York, NY 10016

Distributed in Australia by
Capricorn Link (Australia) Pty Ltd
PO Box 665, Lane Cove, NSW 2066

British Library Cataloguing in Publication Data

Ewart, Ron
The fuchsia grower's handbook.
1. Fuchsias. Cultivation
I. Title
635.9'3344

ISBN 0 7137 1712 2

Typeset by Alden Press (London) Ltd,
Printed in Great Britain by Biddles Ltd., Guildford

Contents

Chapter 1

The History of the Fuchsia

It was in 1703 that the first printed reference to the fuchsia appeared. In that year Father Charles Plumier, a Jesuit monk in the Order of Minims, published his *Nova Plantarum Americanarum Genera.* This was a description of plants which he had discovered in the course of several expeditions on behalf of King Ludwig XIV to the East Indies, Martinique and the West Indies, between 1689 and 1697. It contained a drawing and description of the plant which Plumier called 'Fuchsia triphylla flore coccineo' in honour of a famous sixteenth-century German herbalist, Leonhart Fuchs, sometime Professor of Medicine at the University of Tübingen. Fuchs himself had published a book, *De Historia Stirpium*, and his work was doubtless well known to Plumier.

Plumier did not give in his book the location of his discovery of the fuchsia but it is now generally believed to have been Santo Domingo, for it was there, in 1873, that Thomas Hogg, an American, collected seeds of *F. triphylla* which he sent to New York Botanic Gardens.

Plant collecting expeditions to Central and South America in the latter part of the eighteenth and into the nineteenth centuries discovered and introduced many more new species of fuchsia – *F. magellanica* (1768), *F. coccinea* (1788), *F. lycioides* (1796), *F. arborescens* (1824), *F. microphylla* (1827), *F. fulgens* (1830), *F. corymbiflora* (1840), *F. denticulata (F. serratifolia)* (1844) and *F. boliviana* (1873). The New Zealand species *F. excorticata* was also discovered in 1824.

The first fuchsia believed to have been introduced to Britain is *F. coccinea*, mentioned in *Hortus Kewensis* in 1789. According to *Curtis's Botanical Magazine*, it was first sold in 1792 by James Lee at his Vineyard Nursery in Hammersmith. How it came to be in Lee's possession is uncertain, but it is known that Captain Firth presented a plant of *F. coccinea* to Kew in 1788 and it may be that the plant which Lee had was not *F. coccinea* at all, but *F. magellanica* var. *macrostema* of which *F. coccinea* is a synonym.

With the introduction of so many species into Europe, it was not long before nurserymen and gardeners of the day were trying to raise new hybrids. Felix Porcher, writing in his *Histoire et Culture du Fuchsia*, in 1874, says that the earliest hybrids were raised in England in 1837 from crosses between *F. fulgens* and *F. corymbiflora*, these species being available only in England at that time. It was only after the crossings had been made that these fuchsia hybrids were introduced to the Continent. Early British hybridizers of that era included Harrison, Smith and Standish, and they were soon to be followed by prolific producers of new varieties, such as Banks, Bland, Story and Bull.

In France it was John Salter, an Englishman living in Versailles, who made the earliest crossings and he was soon joined by Dubus, Lemoine, Crousse, Boucharlat the Elder and Baudinat. As the fuchsia spread through Europe, the Belgians and Germans, too, became intent on producing new hybrids and varieties, and the resultant avalanche of new fuchsias appearing in commerce caused Porcher to criticise fiercely those hybridizers who were introducing them, pleading with them to curb their enthusiasm and make sure that the fuchsias had real merit by testing them thoroughly first. Looking at the situation today, nothing has changed.

In 1842 came the first fuchsia with a white tube and sepals – this was 'Venus Victrix', raised by Gulliver, gardener to the Rev. Marriott of Herstmonceux. It figured in the parentage of a large number of new varieties with white tube and sepals and is still extensively used in hybridizing today.

The first varieties were single flowered and it was not until 1850 that the double-flowered varieties appeared, all with red tube and sepals and purple corolla. No parentage is known, but all appeared to have the form of 'Corallina'. In that year Story of Exeter brought out *F. duplex* and *F. multiplex*, but the flowers were so mediocre that they gained no popularity and soon disappeared from cultivation. Some sensation in the horticultural world of the period was caused in 1855 when fuchsias with a white corolla first made their appearance from two British hybridizers, Story, and Luccombe and Pince. Story's 'Queen Victoria' and 'Mrs Story' each had a red tube and sepals with a white corolla and, although their parentage is not known, their appearance opened the doors for a greater variety of colours in the fuchsia than anything up until then.

Fuchsias with a striped corolla, such as 'Striata' (Story 1850), and 'Striata perfecta' (Banks 1856) had great novelty value, as did the first variegated-foliage varieties. The earliest of these was found in Belgium in 1853 and incorrectly named *F. variegata*. The foliage had a yellow variegation but, as the flower had little to commend it, the public took little interest and it disappeared. English growers produced several variegated-leaved varieties in the years from 1865 onwards but only one of these survives today – 'Golden Treasure' from Carter in 1870. Thomas Milner's 'Sunray', introduced in 1872, and still in cultivation, is perhaps the best of the variegated-leaved varieties and vastly superior to the many recent introductions of that type, which are mostly sports.

When early British hybridizers are mentioned, one name stands out far beyond the others; that of James Lye. Lye was head gardener to the Hon. Mrs Hay at Clyffe Hall, Market Lavington in Wiltshire, and in the space of some 25 years he raised over 60 new cultivars, many of which are still grown today. Many of his varieties had the distinct creamy white tube and sepals, which became known as the 'Lye hallmark' and fuchsias such as 'Amy Lye' and 'Lye's Unique' are two first-class examples of that type.

In the latter years of the nineteenth century Lye was also responsible for the production of huge specimen plants – pyramids and pillars – which he would put on display at the horticultural shows in his area, and he was followed by his son-in-law, George Bright of Reading, as an exponent of this unfortunately forgotten art. George Bright's best known introduction was 'Pink Pearl', which came out in 1919 and can still be found in many collections today.

The onset of World War 1 led to a necessity for food production in the large glasshouses previously occupied by fuchsias and interest in the plant declined. Many of the fuchsias raised prior to that time did not survive the war period, although some of the hardy varieties came through unscathed in cottage gardens throughout the UK, and were resurrected in later years when the fuchsia once again regained popularity.

Interest in the fuchsia spread to America in the 1920s, but there were only a few areas where they grew well because of extreme weather conditions. California was one of these areas, and thus cultivation, in the late 1920s and early 1930s, was concentrated there. The American Fuchsia Society was formed in 1929, mainly through the efforts of Miss Alice Eastwood, Curator of Botany at the California Academy of Sciences, and Professor Sydney Mitchell. Professor and Mrs Mitchell visited Britain in 1930 and came to the nursery of H. A. Brown of Chingford to make a selection of fuchsia varieties to be sent to America. A total of some 50 were chosen and it is from these that the majority of American varieties today are descended.

In California there were a number of excellent hybridizers, such as Rieter, Neiderholzer, Hazard, and Lagen, and they were soon to produce well-known fuchsias like 'Cascade', 'Melody', 'Mrs Lovell Swisher', 'R.A.F.' and 'Falling Stars'.

The formation of the British Fuchsia Society, in 1938, was another landmark, the prime movers here being Lady Boothby, Mr W. W. Whiteman and Bert Brown. The latter, now the Rev. Dr Brown, was the son of H. A. Brown, nurseryman at Chingford in East London, who, in order to finance his studies for the ministry (he wanted to become a missionary), took up growing plants as a paying hobby. His first efforts at growing water lilies were none too successful – they took so long to come to maturity and be saleable – so he looked to fuchsias. While success was not immediate, there is no doubt that it was Bert Brown's interest in fuchsias, and the displays which he put on at Chelsea and elsewhere in those years just prior to World War 2, that spawned a wider interest in this plant, which had almost sunk into oblivion, and helped it to rise once again up the popularity ladder to where it is today.

The fuchsia's success was also Bert Brown's success, for he sailed through college and went off as a missionary to Papua New Guinea where he has spent most of his life since, returning from time to time to Britain where his sisters, Margaret and Edith, still run the Chingford Nursery.

Since World War 2 the fuchsia has gained in popularity and hybridizers are working in many countries throughout the world in an attempt to bring out new and better varieties. Fuchsia societies are now found worldwide, local societies are being formed with great regularity in Britain, and there is a tremendous spirit of fellowship reigning in the fuchsia world. The phrase 'fuchsia folk are friendly folk' is just as true today as when it was first coined – one can only wonder if Père Plumier knew what he was starting away back in 1703.

Chapter 2

Propagation

Fuchsias can be propagated in several ways – by seeds, cuttings, grafts and mutations. Seed propagation is dealt with on page 27, so here I will only deal with the other methods.

Cuttings

Cuttings can be softwood, semi-hardwood or hardwood, but the first is the most common method.

They may be taken at any time of the year when suitable stock is available, but for the amateur grower spring is the best time as it is then that growth is strongest and growing conditions best. Light, warmth and moisture are the three essentials for good growth, and if all of these are available then success is assured.

There are numerous proprietary brands of compost now available for seed sowing and for cuttings, but all that is necessary is a 50/50 mixture of moss peat and sharp grit or sand, or peat and perlite. A standard seed tray will comfortably hold 48 cuttings, and a half tray 24. The compost should be firmed into the tray, then watered and allowed to drain before the cuttings are inserted.

The cutting itself should be small, two pairs of leaves and the growing tip, carefully removed from the parent plant with a clean knife or other sharp instrument, just below a node (Fig. 1).

This is then carefully inserted into the compost, using a small split cane to make the hole and so avoid damage to the stem of the cutting. The use of rooting hormone powders is completely unnecessary with fuchsias, as these tend to delay rather than assist

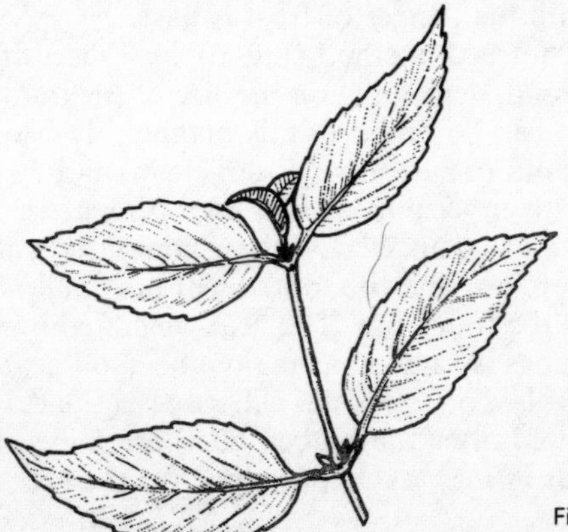

Fig. 1 A cutting

rooting. When the tray has been filled, and all the cuttings labelled, a light mist spray can be given before the tray is covered, either with one of the plastic domes which are sold in most garden shops as propagator tops and will cover either size of seed tray, or with a plastic cover held up by wire hoops to keep it from coming into contact with the cuttings. Where cuttings are taken in January or early February, bottom heat, to give a temperature of 18°C (65°F) is needed, but where this is not available it is better to delay taking cuttings until late February or March, when the air temperature in the greenhouse has gone up to over 10°C (50°F).

In a cold greenhouse, where there is no artificial heat, the cuttings should not be taken until April.

Watch the cuttings carefully, ensuring that any dead leaves are quickly removed to avoid the growth of botrytis. When they show signs of having rooted, give a little ventilation by lifting the ends of the plastic cover, or opening the vents on the top of the dome. Rooting time depends greatly on the temperature available and can be from ten days to three or four weeks, according to the time of year, but, when the young cuttings appear to be growing strongly, they should be carefully removed from the propagator and potted up individually into small pots of no more than 5 cm (2 in) diameter. The compost for these should be either a John Innes No 1 or any soil-less compost.

The cuttings, once potted up, should be placed out of direct sunlight for a few days until they have settled into their new environment. Their subsequent care is dealt with in later chapters.

Where cuttings of a particular variety are scarce, it is possible to make several cuttings out of one small piece (Fig. 2). These are treated just like normal cuttings, but, being small, care must be taken not to overwater them in the early stages.

For the grower without a greenhouse, cuttings can be rooted easily on a light windowsill in either trays or pots, but do ensure that they are not in full sun.

Cold frames are also useful, although cuttings should not be struck in a frame until the danger of frost is past.

I have found the 'hot bed' method (Fig. 3) very successful. This utilises a cold frame and, depending on the size of the frame, many hundreds of cuttings can be raised in this manner, The soil in the frame should be dug out to a depth of 45 cm (18 in) and the bottom 30 cm (12 in) filled with either pine needles or rotting grass cuttings, well rammed down and compacted. This is copiously watered to assist in the rotting process and the subsequent heat build-up, then soil is added to level the frame out. The heat generated by the pine needles or grass cuttings is as good as many undersoil heaters, and cuttings struck in trays laid on top of this will root very quickly. A few days should be allowed after the hotbed has been laid before the cuttings are put in, as it does take a little time for the heat to build up.

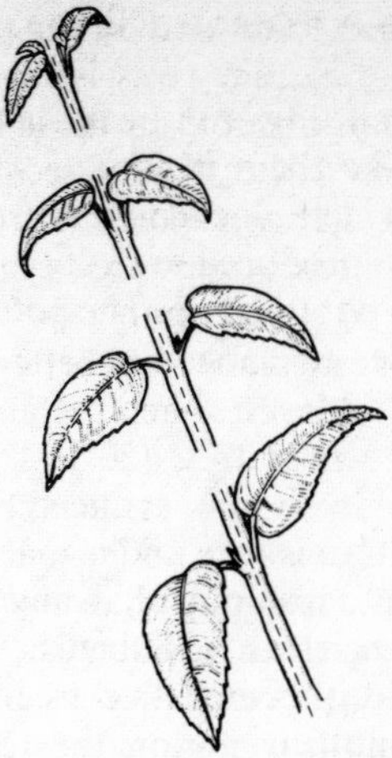

Fig. 2 Multiple cuttings from one small piece of material

The biennial method of cultivation, mainly used by those who grow for exhibition, requires cuttings to be taken in June and July and this is dealt with in Chapter 9.

Semi-hardwood cuttings may be taken in autumn, but it is a prerequisite of autumn cuttings that sufficient heat must be available to keep them growing throughout the winter months. A temperature of 7°C (45°F) is sufficient for this purpose and will keep the young plants ticking over while not making any great amount of growth.

Hardwood cuttings are rarely used, although I have employed this method with 30 cm (12 in) pieces cut from hardy garden fuchsias such as *F. magellanica* var. *macrostema* and *F. m. alba*. These were placed in bundles, 15 cm (6 in) deep, in a sheltered corner of the

Fig. 3 'Hot bed' method using a cold frame

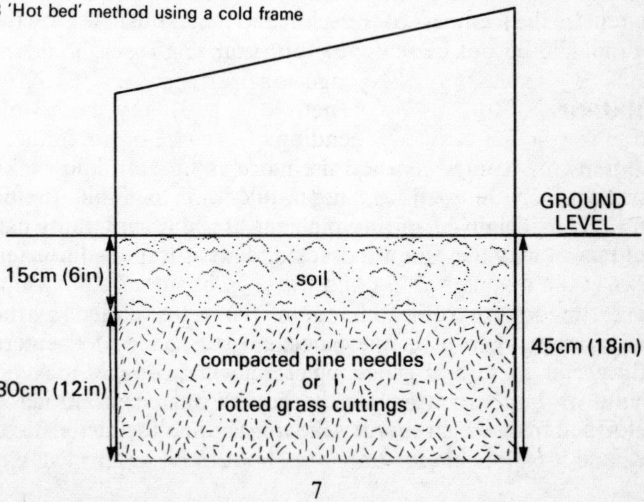

garden in October in the same way as one would root privet cuttings, with reasonable success.

It is safe to say that fuchsia cuttings can be rooted in almost any medium and many people strike them in jars of water on a windowsill. The only problem which one can encounter with this method is that the 'water roots' produced are very brittle and easily broken when the time comes to pot them up. The pots of rooting gel, which are now widely available, give a similar type of root.

Grafts

The use of grafts in fuchsia culture is rare and is mainly undertaken for the purpose of making standards out of varieties too weak to make a strong enough stem themselves. Whether the grafting of one or more different varieties onto one single stem can be said to be more than just a novelty is doubtful.

The stock should be selected from one of the stronger, fast growing varieties – 'Phyllis', 'Mrs Lovell Swisher', 'Checkerboard' or 'Celia Smedley' are all eminently suitable – and it should be grown up over a year to make a good straight stem with the leaves left on.

The scion should be of semi-hardwood and not too large, three to four pairs of leaves being sufficient, remembering that it is likely to take three to four weeks before the graft takes.

The best time of year for this operation is probably the spring, when growth is strongest, and the easiest method is the one known as 'saddle grafting'.

To prepare for the graft, the standard is cut back to the required height and an incision made on the top to a depth of approximately 2 cm ($\frac{3}{4}$ in). The base of the scion is also trimmed to shape and inserted into the stock. The graft is then tied in with raffia and the plant left in a cool place out of direct sunlight until the graft has taken. As with cuttings, the fact that the union has taken will be apparent by the freshness of the scion and it making new growth, but the raffia should not be removed too soon.

Mutations

Mutations, or 'sports' as they are more commonly known, occur very frequently in fuchsias, and while it is possible to induce mutations artificially by means of chemical and other treatments, the exact reason why they should occur under natural conditions is not known.

Mutation results from a change in the genes, either in a single gene, where a change in one particular character of the plant is produced, or in several genes, where marked changes may occur. Somatic or bud mutations may arise in cells from which buds develop and from which shoots, showing the new characteristics, will grow, and it is possible for only one shoot to be so affected, e.g. on a plant with normal green leaves, one shoot with leaf variegations may appear. In fuchsias the most common mutations one finds are (a) variegated foliage on a normally green-leaved plant, and (b) a change in flower colour. In recent years numerous variegated mutations of established varieties have occurred and in most the new characteristics have remained fixed, as have the flower colour changes. Propagation of mutated shoots is done by cuttings, and the resultant plants should be carefully watched for several years to ensure that reversion does not occur.

Chapter 3

The Fuchsia Species

The genus Fuchsia is divided into nine sections and there are, in all, just over 100 different species known to be in cultivation at present.

1 Section Quelusia

Found in Argentina, Brazil and Chile. The tube is usually not longer than the sepals and the stamens are long and exserted.

F. bracelinae
Tube dark red, short.
Sepals rose, short, held well out.
Corolla purple, short.
Foliage medium sized, green on top and reddish on the underside, slightly serrated.
Growth very low growing, shrubby.

F. campus-portoi
Tube and sepals red, short.
Corolla violet purple, small.
Foliage reddish-green, small, serrated.
Growth upright, shrubby.

F. coccinea
Tube and sepals red. Sepals long and narrow.
Corolla violet purple, small.
Foliage small and broad, medium green on top, paler green on the undersides.
Growth upright, bushy and fairly vigorous.

F. magellanica
Tube deep red, short and slender.
Sepals deep red, short, medium width and held well out.
Corolla opening bright purple, fading as the bloom matures.
Foliage darkish green, usually with reddish veins. Leaves opposite or ternate, lanceolate to ovate, serrated and with short petioles.
Growth shrubby, up to 12 ft (3.5 m) in height. Free branching with slender, reddish shoots.

F. magellanica var. *magellanica*
Similar to *F. magellanica* except that the leaves are slightly smaller and the corolla a less bright shade of purple.

F. magellanica var. ***alba***
(Syn. *F. magellanica* var. *molinae*)
Tube and sepals pink.
Corolla lilac pink, small and compact.
Stamens and style pink
Foliage pale to medium green, small and serrated.
Growth upright and bushy, to 12 ft (3.7 m)

F. magellanica var. ***macrostema***
(Syn. *F. coccinea* [Curtis]
F. gracilis var. *macrostema* [Lindley]
F. gracilis [Lindley]
F. magellanica var. *gracilis* [Bailey])
Tube red, short and slender.
Sepals red.
Corolla purplish. Small, fairly compact blooms.
Foliage darkish green, small and serrated.
Growth upright, bushy and vigorous.

F. regia
Tube deep red.
Sepals red, long and narrow, held well out.

Corolla purplish, short and compact.
Foliage darkish green with red veins. Leaves small and narrow, opposite or ternate, serrated and often pilose.
Growth upright, shrubby, free branching with slender reddish branches. Grows up to 20 ft (6 m).

F. regia* var. *alpestris
Colour as for F. regia.
Leaves and young branches pilose.
Foliage and growth as for *F. regia*. Fairly hardy.

F. regia* var. *regia
Colour as for *F. regia*
Foliage and branches devoid of hair.
Growth as for *F. regia*.

2 Section Fuchsia

Found in the Andes and Central America. The tube is several times as long as the sepals and the stamens do not extend much beyond the petals.

F. abrupta
Tube bright orange, shiny, bulbous at the base, long and slender.
Sepals bright, shiny orange, held well out from the corolla.
Corolla small, orange red. Flowers in racemes.
Foliage medium to large, dark green, heavily veined.
Growth shrubby upright, to 10 ft (3 m).

F. ampliata
Tube scarlet to orange red, thin at the top becoming more bulbous at the base.
Sepals scarlet to orange red, small to medium size, reflexing to the tube as the bloom matures.
Corolla orange red, small and compact.
Foliage matt green on the upper surface with stiff bristly hair, paler green on the underside. Reddish-purple veins.
Growth shrubby upright to 10 ft (3 m).

F. andrei
Tube orange red to coral red, medium length.
Sepals orange to coral red, small.
Corolla orange red, small and compact. Flowers in racemes.
Ecuador and Peru.

F. austromontana
Tube scarlet, longish and narrow.
Sepals small, scarlet. Held well out as the bloom matures.
Corolla deep red, compact but opening out with age.
Foliage dark green on top, paler green and pilose on the underside. Leaves medium to largish, slightly serrated.
Growth upright to 13 ft (4 m). Axillary flowering.
Bolivia and Peru.

F. ayavacensis
Tube orange red, thin, medium length, bulbous at the base.
Sepals orange red, small, held horizontally.
Corolla small, orange red.
Foliage fairly large, matt green on top, lighter green and pilose on the underside and slightly serrated.
Growth upright to 13 ft (4 m).
Ecuador and Peru.

F. boliviana
Tube scarlet to dark red, long, up to 2 in (6 cm).
Sepals scarlet to dark red, reflexing as the bloom matures.
Corolla scarlet, small.
Foliage light to medium green, medium to large.
Growth upright and shrubby. Flowers in terminal racemes. Can be distinguished from *F. corymbiflora* (q.v.) by the reflexing sepals.
Bolivia, Argentina and Peru.

F. canescens

Tube dull red, medium length, bulbous at the base.

Sepals scarlet, greenish tips, short and held well out.

Corolla dark red, small, opening as the bloom matures.

Foliage medium green on top, lighter on the underside with reddish veins. Medium size.

Growth shrubby, upright to 13 ft (4 m).

Colombia.

F. caucana

Tube cerise pink to lavender purple, thin at the top becoming bulbous towards the base, longish.

Sepals same colour as the tube, short and spreading.

Corolla dark reddish-purple, spreading as the bloom ages.

Foliage dark green on top, pale greenish-white on the underside, medium sized and serrated.

Growth upright to 6 ft (2 m).

Colombia.

F. ceracea

Tube bright pink to lavender, narrow, longish, becoming bulbous towards the base.

Sepals pink to lavender, medium length, held down over the corolla.

Corolla crimson to purple, small and compact.

Foliage medium green with reddish stems. Medium-sized waxy leaves.

Growth shrubby upright to 16 ft (5 m). Axillary flowering.

Ecuador and Colombia.

F. cochabambana

Tube orange red, long and narrow, bulbous at the base.

Sepals orange red to crimson, medium sized.

Corolla red, small and compact.

Foliage medium green, flushed purple and pilose on the underside. Medium to large sized.

Growth shrubby upright to 5 ft (1.5 m). Flowers axillary.

Bolivia.

F. concertifolia

Tube red, narrow and longish. Slightly bulbous at the base.

Sepals red, small and narrow.

Corolla red, small.

Foliage medium green, very small. Stems reddish and pilose.

Growth vigorous shrub, to 8 ft (2.5 m).

Peru.

F. coriacifolia

Tube, sepals and corolla rose pink.

Foliage dark green on top, paler whitish-green on the underside with red veins.

Growth shrubby, upright to 6 ft (2 m).

Peru.

F. corollata

Tube shiny reddish-pink to scarlet, longish and narrow, bulbous at the base.

Sepals pale scarlet with greenish tips. Medium sized, spreading out horizontally.

Corolla scarlet, small.

Foliage dark shiny green on top, paler on the undersides. Leaves medium sized with reddish veins.

Growth upright climber to 16 ft (5 m). Flowers axillary.

Colombia and Ecuador.

F. corymbiflora

Tube scarlet, long – 2 in (6 cm).

Sepals scarlet, small, spreading slightly from the corolla.

Corolla darker shade of scarlet, small, opening out as the bloom ages.

Foliage matt green on top, lighter on the undersides, medium to largish sized.

Growth upright, shrubby to 13 ft (4 m). Flowers in terminal racemes.

Peru.

F. crassistipula

Tube pinkish-scarlet, long and thin, broadening towards the base.

Sepals pinkish-scarlet, deeper at the tips, short and narrow and held down over the corolla.

Corolla darker red, small and compact, opening up as the bloom ages.
Foliage dark green on top, paler on the underside with a purplish flush. Leaves medium to long with serrated edges.
Colombia.

F. cautrecasii
Tube shiny orange red, long and narrow.
Sepals shiny orange red, small to medium sized.
Corolla orange red, small and compact, opening as the flower matures.
Foliage darkish glossy green with a purple tinge on the undersides.
Growth low shrub to 5 ft (1.5 m). Flowers in short terminal racemes.
Colombia.

F. decussata
Tube reddish, narrow, medium length.
Sepals red with green tips. Small, held well out when the flower matures.
Corolla scarlet to reddish-orange, small.
Foliage dark green on top, paler on the undersides with reddish hairs on the veins. Leaves small.
Growth upright, climbing shrub to 10 ft (3 m). Flowers axillary.
Peru.

F. denticulata
(Syn. *F. serratifolia.*)
Tube light red, narrow, longish and slightly pilose.
Sepals red with greenish-white tips, held well out over the corolla.
Corolla orange to scarlet, smallish and fairly compact.
Foliage dark shiny green on top, paler on the underside with a reddish flush.
Growth upright, shrubby to 13 ft (4 m). Axillary flowers.
Peru and Bolivia.

F. dependens
Tube reddish-orange to scarlet, narrow and longish, pilose on the outside.
Sepals reddish-orange with green tips, small and held well out.
Corolla orange red, small.
Foliage dull green on top, paler on the undersides with a reddish centre vein. Leaves medium sized and longish.
Growth upright, shrubby with arching branches to 33 ft (10 m). Flowers in terminal racemes.
Colombia and Ecuador.

F. ferreyrae
Tube dark reddish-violet, thin, medium length, slightly bulbous at the base.
Sepals dark reddish-violet, medium length, spreading.
Corolla reddish-violet, small.
Foliage dark velvety green on top, tinged bluish on the undersides. Leaves medium sized with serrated edges.
Growth shrubby upright to 10 ft (3 m).
Peru.

F. fontinalis
Tube shiny reddish-pink, medium length, narrow and bulbous at the base.
Sepals shiny reddish-pink, small and held well out.
Corolla red, small.
Foliage darkish green red stems.
Growth upright, spreading, to 13 ft (4 m). Axillary flowers, or sometimes in racemes or panicles.
Peru.

F. furfuracea
Tube pinkish-lavender, longish and narrow.
Sepals light red, whitish at the tips. Small and held well out.
Corolla bright reddish-pink to dark red, small.
Foliage dark green on top, lighter green on the underside with a purplish tinge. Leaves medium to large and serrated.
Growth upright, climbing shrub to 7 ft (2.5 m).
Bolivia.

F. gehrigeri
Tube shiny red, long and narrow, bulbous at the base.
Sepals shiny red, medium size and held well out from the corolla.
Corolla scarlet, small to medium size.
Foliage deep matt green on top, paler on the underside with a purplish tinge. Veins pilose. Leaves medium to large.
Growth upright, climbing shrub to 16 ft (5 m). Flowers axillary.
Venezuela and Colombia.

F. glaberrima
Tube orange red to red, narrow and longish.
Sepals orange red to red, small and held well out.
Corolla red, small and compact.
Foliage green, pilose, reddish-violet flush on the underside.
Leaves large.
Growth upright to 10 ft (3 m). Flowers in terminal racemes.
Ecuador and Peru.

F. harlingii
Tube pale reddish-orange, medium length and thickness.
Sepals pale reddish-orange, short, held out over the corolla.
Corolla red, small and compact.
Foliage darkish green on top, paler on the underside. Leaves small and stems purplish.
Growth upright, climbing to 10 ft (3 m). Axillary flowering.
Ecuador.

F. hartwegii
Tube reddish-orange, long and narrow, bulbous at the base.
Sepals reddish-orange, small and held well out from the corolla.
Corolla red, small and compact.
Foliage dark green on top, paler on the underside with reddish veins. Leaves large.
Growth upright, climbing shrub to 13 ft (4 m), flowering mostly in racemes.
Colombia.

F. hirtella
Tube lavender to reddish-pink, long and narrow, bulbous at the base.
Sepals lavender to reddish-pink, medium length, tapering, held well out.
Corolla crimson, small.
Foliage dark green on top, lighter on the underside. Leaves longish and slightly serrated.
Growth upright, climbing shrub to 16 ft (5 m).
Colombia.

F. lehmanii
Tube orange to coral red, medium length, thin and bulbous at the base.
Sepals orange to coral red, shiny, narrow and reflexing slightly.
Corolla orange red, small, opening out as the bloom matures.
Foliage dark green on top, paler on the underside. Leaves medium sized.
Growth upright, climbing to 10 ft (3 m).
Ecuador.

F. llewelynii
Tube pink, long and thin, slightly bulbous at the base.
Sepals pink, small and narrow.
Corolla pink, small.
Foliage medium green, heavily serrated. Leaves medium sized and stems spiny.
Growth shrubby, low growing.
Peru.

F. loxensis
Tube bright scarlet, medium length, narrow and slightly bulbous at the base.
Sepals scarlet, small and narrow, held well out and reflexing slightly as the bloom matures.
Corolla small, dull red.
Foliage deep shiny green with reddish veins on the underside.
Leaves medium sized.
Growth upright and bushy. Axillary flowering.
Ecuador.

F. macropetala

Tube bright red, long and narrow.
Sepals bright red, small and held well out.
Corolla red, small and compact.
Foliage large, medium green, flushed purple on the underside with reddish veins.
Growth upright, shrubby or climbing, to 10 ft (3 m).
Peru.

F. macrophylla

Tube red, medium length.
Sepals red with green tips, small.
Corolla bright scarlet red, small and compact.
Foliage dark green on top, paler green underneath with reddish veins. Leaves large, up to 6 in (15 cm) long.
Growth shrubby upright. Young branches have a reddish-purple tinge.
Peru.

F. macrostigma

Tube red, long and narrow, bulbous at the base.
Sepals red with green tips, medium sized and held well out.
Corolla bright red, small and loose.
Foliage dark velvety green on top and pilose, paler green with a purplish flush on the underside. Leaf size varies from medium to very large, up to 9 in (23 cm) long.
Growth upright, shrubby to 5 ft (1.5 m).
Colombia and Ecuador.

F. magdalenae

(Syn. *F. lampadaria.*)
Tube bright orange red, purplish at the base. Long and thickish but wider at the base.
Sepals bright orange red with green tips, medium length, spreading as the bloom matures.
Corolla orange red, medium size.
Foliage dark green on top, lighter on the underside with purplish veins. Leaves medium to large and slightly serrated.
Growth shrubby upright to 16 ft (5 m). Young growth purplish.
Colombia.

F. mathewsii

Tube pale lavender to pink, long and narrow, slightly bulbous at the base.
Sepals light red, medium size, held well out.
Corolla crimson red to light purple, small and loose.
Foliage dark green on top and covered with fine hairs, lighter green on the underside with reddish hairs. Large leaves.
Growth shrubby upright to 10 ft (3 m).
Peru.

F. nigricans

Tube light red, long and of medium thickness, slightly broader at the base.
Sepals light red, short and held well out over the corolla.
Corolla medium to dark purple, small and fairly compact but opening as the bloom matures.
Foliage darkish green on top, lighter on the underside. Medium sized leaves.
Growth upright and shrubby, to 10 ft (3 m).
Venezuela and Colombia.

F. orientalis

Tube scarlet to reddish-orange, long and narrow, slightly bulbous at the base.
Sepals scarlet to reddish-orange, small.
Corolla red to orange red, small and compact.
Foliage mid-green on top, lighter on the underside, veins pilose.
Leaves medium to large, up to 9 in (23 cm).
Growth upright and shrubby to 6 ft (2 m). Flowers in axillary racemes.
Ecuador.

F. ovalis

Tube red, long and narrow, bulbous

at the base.
Sepals red, small and narrow.
Corolla red, small.
Foliage dark green on top, lighter on the underside, veins pilose. Pedicels long and pilose.
Growth upright and shrubby to 10 ft (3 m).
Peru.

F. pallescens
Tube pink to pale red, shiny, medium length and thickness, slightly pilose.
Sepals pink to pale red, medium length, narrow and held well out.
Corolla dark red to maroon, small.
Foliage dark velvety green and pilose on the upper surface, lighter green on the underside with veins pilose. Leaves small to medium sized.
Growth low growing shrub.
Ecuador and Colombia.

F. petiolaris
Tube shiny rose pink, long and narrow, slightly bulbous at the base.
Sepals shiny rose pink with green tips, long, narrow and flaring out from the corolla.
Corolla bright reddish-pink, finely pilose on the backs of the petals, medium to small and fairly loose.
Foliage mid-green on top, paler green on the underside. Leaves medium sized and covered in fine hairs.
Growth upright shrub or climber to 6 ft (2 m).
Venezuela and Colombia.

F. pilosa
Tube bright orange red, medium length.
Sepals bright orange red, small and narrow, recurving slightly.
Corolla orange red, small and loose.
Foliage matt green on top, paler green on the underside. Leaves medium to large and covered in long hairs.
Stems and flowers finely pilose. Flowers in terminal racemes.
Growth upright and shrubby to 6 ft (2 m).
Peru.

F. polyantha
Tube red, long and narrow.
Sepals red, medium length, narrow.
Corolla slightly darker shade of red, small.
Foliage dark shiny green on top, lighter green on the underside with veins pilose. Leaves medium to large.
Growth upright, shrubby to 6 ft (2 m).
Ecuador.

F. pringsheimii
Tube pinkish-red to bright red, medium width, long.
Sepals pinkish-red to bright red, long and narrow, held well out as the bloom matures.
Corolla pinkish-red to red, medium size, petals roll up as they mature.
Foliage glossy dark green on top, greenish-white on the underside with a purplish flush and reddish-purple veins. Slightly pilose.
Leaves small.
Growth upright and shrubby to 6 ft (2 m).
Dominica and Haiti.

F. putumayensis
Tube shiny orange red or coral red, long and narrow, finely pilose on the outside.
Sepals orange red to coral red, small and narrow, curling slightly.
Corolla orange red, small and loose.
Foliage matt green and pilose on top, paler green and finely pilose on the underside. Leaves medium to large.
Growth shrubby and upright to 10 ft (3 m).
Ecuador and Colombia.

F. rivularis
Tube bright scarlet, very long and narrow, bulbous at the base.
Sepals bright scarlet, long and narrow.

Corolla orange red, medium sized and loose-petalled.
Foliage shiny dark green on top, lighter green and finely pilose on the underside. Leaves medium sized.
Growth climbing shrub with long, slender branches to 30 ft (10 m).
Peru.

F. sanctae-rosea
Tube shiny reddish-orange, narrow, medium length.
Sepals shiny orange red, short and narrow, held well out.
Corolla scarlet to orange red, small and loose-petalled.
Foliage deep green on top, paler on the underside. Leaves medium sized and finely pilose.
Growth shrubby upright to 10 ft (3 m). Young branches reddish-purple.
Bolivia and Peru.

F. sanmartina
Tube bright red, very long (3 in/75 mm) and narrow, wider at the base and finely pilose.
Sepals bright red, long and narrow.
Corolla red, smallish.
Foliage mid-green, medium to large leaves, finely pilose.
Growth climbing shrub to 10 ft (3 m). Flowers in terminal racemes.
Peru.

F. scabriuscula
Tube pinkish-white to red, medium length, narrow at the top and wider at the base.
Sepals reddish, short and narrow, held well out.
Corolla reddish-pink, small and loose-petalled.
Foliage dull green on top, heavily veined, paler green on the underside with a purple flush. Medium sized leaves with pilose petioles. Axillary flowering.
Growth low creeping shrub.
Colombia and Ecuador.

F. scherffiana
Tube orange red, long and narrow with a slightly bulbous base.
Sepals orange red, short and narrow, held well out.
Corolla red, small.
Foliage dark shiny green on top, shiny green with a purple flush on the underside and pilose. Leaves medium sized.
Growth upright and shrubby to 10 ft (3 m). Stems purplish. Axillary flowering.
Ecuador.

F. sessilifolia
Tube greenish-red, medium length.
Sepals greenish-red, small and narrow and held well out.
Corolla scarlet, small and loose-petalled.
Foliage shiny dark green on top, paler green with a purplish flush and finely pilose on the underside.
Growth upright and shrubby to 10 ft (3 m). Young branches reddish and finely pilose. Flowers in terminal racemes.
Colombia and Ecuador.

F. simplicicaulis
Tube pale reddish-pink, long and bulbous, finely pilose.
Sepals pale reddish-pink, long and narrow.
Corolla red, small.
Foliage medium green and pilose. Leaves medium to large.
Growth climbing shrub up to 16 ft (5 m). Flowers in racemes.
Peru.

F. steyermarkii
Tube rose red, long, narrow at the top and wider at the base.
Sepals rose red, long and narrow.
Corolla scarlet, small.
Foliage dark green on top, lighter on the underside and pilose.
Leaves medium sized.
Growth shrubby upright to 6 ft (2 m). Branches pilose.
Ecuador.

F. sylvatica
Tube rose red, medium length, narrow at the top and wider at the base.
Sepals rose red to red, medium length, narrow and held well out from the corolla.
Corolla crimson red, small.
Foliage darkish green on top, lighter green with a reddish flush on the underside. Leaves medium sized.
Growth upright climbing shrub to 8 ft (2.5 m).
Ecuador.

F. tincta
Tube pinkish-red, medium length, narrow at the top and widening towards the base.
Sepals pinkish-red, short and narrow, held well out.
Corolla reddish-pink, small and loose-petalled.
Foliage dark green on top, lighter green with a purplish flush on the undersides. Veins pilose. Leaves medium to large.
Growth upright, low growing shrub to 5 ft (1.5 m). Young stems whitish and pilose. Flowers in terminal racemes.
Peru.

F. triphylla
Tube orange red to coral red, medium length, thin at the top becoming bulbous.
Sepals orange red to coral red, short and stubby, held well down.
Corolla orange to coral red, small and compact.
Foliage dull darkish green on top, lighter on the underside with reddish veins and a purplish flush.
Growth shrubby, low growing with reddish pilose young growth.
Haiti, Dominica and Hispaniola.

F. vargasiana
Tube red, medium length, thin at the top and widening towards the base.
Sepals red at the base, green tips, small and narrow, held well out.
Corolla red, small and loose-petalled.
Foliage dark shiny green on top, paler on the underside. Leaves medium to large.
Growth upright and shrubby to 6 ft (2 m). Flowers in terminal racemes.
Peru.

F. venusta
Tube shiny orange red, long, thin at the top and widening towards the base.
Sepals orange red with green tips, medium length, narrow and held well out.
Corolla reddish-orange to orange, small to medium size and loose-petalled.
Foliage dark glossy green on top, pale green on the underside.
Leaves medium to large.
Growth upright climbing shrub to 10 ft (3 m). Stems bluish-purple. Axillary flowering.
Venezuela and Colombia.

F. verrucosa
Tube bright reddish-orange, small and thick.
Sepals reddish-orange, small and recurving.
Corolla reddish-orange, small.
Foliage matt green on top, paler green with a purplish flush on the underside. Leaves medium to large.
Growth upright climbing shrub to 6 ft (2 m). Axillary flowering.
Colombia and Venezuela.

F. vulcanica
Tube shiny scarlet to orange, long, thin at the top and wider at the base. Pilose inside and out.
Sepals shiny scarlet to orange with green tips. Longish and narrow, held well out.
Corolla red, small to medium sized, loose-petalled.
Foliage shiny green on top, lighter on the underside. Leaves medium sized and pilose.
Growth upright climbing shrub to 11 ft (3.5 m). Branches and stems pilose. Axillary flowering.
Ecuador and Colombia.

F. wurdackii
Tube coral red, long and narrow, bulbous at the base and pilose on the outside.
Sepals coral red, short and broad, held well out.
Corolla red, small to medium size.
Foliage medium green and pilose. Leaves medium to large.
Growth upright and shrubby to 5 ft (1.5 m). Young growth finely pilose.
Peru.

3 Section Kierschlegeria

Chile. The leaves have a thickened persistent petiole which becomes spine-like. The petals are the same length, or almost as long, as the sepals which are reflexed. Leaves are mostly opposite or in whorls, and the flowers are small.

F. lycioides
Tube red, very small.
Sepals red, small and reflexing slightly.
Corolla purplish, small.
Foliage dark green on top, paler on the underside, very small. When the leaves are shed the thickened woody bases of the petioles form spines 1.5–2 mm long.
Growth upright and shrubby. Axillary flowering.
Chile.

4 Section Skinnera

New Zealand and Tahiti. Sepals are reflexed, petals are very small or lacking, and leaves are alternate.

F. colensoi
Tube red, small.
Sepals greenish to reddish, small. Spreading and slightly reflexing.
Corolla purple, short and small.
Foliage green on top, whitish on the underside, the main veins pilose.
Growth shrubby upright.
A F. perscandens × F. excorticata natural hybrid.
New Zealand.

F. cyrtandroides
Tube rose magenta, short and narrow, thickening slightly from the base.
Sepals rose magenta, small, narrow and spreading.
Corolla rose magenta, small.
Foliage green on top, white on the underside. Large leaves.
Growth upright, shrubby to 16 ft (5 m).
Tahiti.

F. excorticata
Tube green, becoming dark reddish-purple. Short.
Sepals green, becoming reddish-purple, short and slightly reflexed.
Corolla dark purple with blue anthers and yellowish stigma.
Foliage green on top, whitish on the underside with pilose veining. Leaves medium sized.
Growth upright, bushy and spreading. Bark light brown and papery. Axillary flowering.
New Zealand.

F. perscandens
Tube red, small.
Sepals greenish to reddish, small.
Corolla purple, small and compact.
Foliage green on top, whitish on the underside. Leaves small.
Growth climbing shrub. Small flowers.
New Zealand.

F. procumbens
Tube yellowish-green, red at the base, short and stubby.
Sepals chocolate brown, very small.
Corolla lacking.
Foliage darkish green on top, lighter on the underside, very small, cordate.
Growth trailer with thin, wiry stems. Flowers held upright and the large berries maturing to plum purple.
New Zealand.

5 Section Hemsleyella

Peru, Bolivia and Venezuela. Petals very small or lacking. Tuberous stems. Flowering usually takes place when the plant is leafless.

F. apetala
Tube rose red to light orange red, long (up to 6 in/15 cm).
Sepals rose red, short and stubby.
Corolla lacking.
Foliage green on top, whitish on the underside and pilose. Leaves medium to large.
Growth trailing or epiphytic.
Peru and Bolivia.

F. cestroides
Tube rose pink, short and narrow, widening slightly from the base.
Sepals greenish to purple, short and stubby.
Corolla lacking.
Foliage green on top, lighter on the underside, medium-sized leaves with pilose veining.
Growth upright, shrubby to 10 ft (3 m). Flowers in axillary or terminal racemes.
Peru.

F. chloroloba
Tube orange pink to scarlet, thin at the base and widening.
Sepals bright green, short and stubby.
Corolla lacking.
Foliage green on top, lighter underneath. Medium to large leaves.
Growth upright and shrubby to 6 ft (2 m).
Peru.

F. garleppiana
Tube pale pink, long, narrow and bulbous at the base.
Sepals small, pale pink.
Corolla lacking.
Foliage pale green on top, lighter underneath, veins pilose.
Growth shrubby upright to 13 ft (4 m). Axillary flowering.
Bolivia.

F. huanucoensis
Tube magenta, longish, narrow at the base and widening towards the rim.
Sepals magenta, small and narrow.
Corolla lacking.
Foliage dark green on top, paler on the undersides, veins pilose.
Growth low-growing shrub. Axillary flowering.
Peru.

F. inflata
Tube pale pink to orange, longish and fairly thick.
Sepals pale yellowish-green, short and reflexing.
Corolla lacking.
Foliage green on top, lighter underneath. Medium-sized leaves.
Growth shrubby upright to 10 ft (3 m). Flowers axillary.
Peru.

F. insignis
Tube bright orange red, long, narrow and bulbous at the base.
Sepals bright orange red, medium length and narrow, recurving slightly.
Corolla lacking.
Foliage green on top, paler green on the undersides with purplish flush.

Growth low growing or epiphytic shrub.
Ecuador.

F. juntasensis
Tube deep lavender to rosy violet, long and narrow but widening towards the rim.
Sepals deep lavender to rosy violet, medium length and narrow, recurving slightly.
Corolla lacking.
Foliage green on top, purplish tinge on the underside. Medium-sized leaves.
Growth climbing, mostly epiphytic, up to 50 cm in height.
Bolivia.

F. membranacea
Tube reddish-pink, medium length, becoming bulbous at the rim.
Sepals greenish, short, held well out as the bloom matures.
Corolla lacking.
Foliage shiny green on top, paler on the underside, medium-sized leaves.
Growth upright shrub to 6 ft (2 m) or epiphytic to 33 ft (10 m). Axillary flowering.
Venezuela.

F. nana
Tube bright reddish-pink, short, bulbous at the base.
Sepals bright reddish-pink, short and recurving.
Corolla lacking.
Foliage green on top, lighter on the undersides with a purplish tinge.
Growth trailing shrub. Axillary flowering.
Bolivia.

F. pilaloensis
Tube pale pink, medium thickness, bulbous at the base.
Sepals whitish to pale pink, short and broad.
Corolla lacking.
Foliage green on top, paler on the undersides.
Growth low growing shrub to 3 ft (1 m) or epiphytic to 25 ft (8 m). Flowers axillary.
Ecuador.

F. salicifolia
Tube reddish-pink, bulbous at the base and widening towards the rim. Medium length.
Sepals paler reddish-pink, short and narrow, spreading.
Corolla lacking.
Foliage pale green on top, lighter green with a purplish tinge on the underside. Medium-sized leaves, long and narrow.
Growth epiphytic. Axillary flowering.
Peru and Bolivia.

F. tillettiana
Tube rose pink to cerise, bulbous at the base and widening towards the rim, longish.
Sepals rose pink to cerise, narrow and reflexing.
Corolla lacking.
Foliage green on top, lighter on the underside, medium-sized leaves.
Growth low-growing shrub to 6 ft (2 m) or epiphytic to 30 ft (10 m).
Venezuela.

F. tunariensis
Tube reddish-pink to pale orange, short and stubby.
Sepals reddish-pink to pale orange, short, broad and recurving.
Corolla lacking.
Foliage green on top, paler on the underside. Medium-sized leaves.
Growth low-growing shrub to 4 ft (1.5 m). Axillary flowering.
Peru and Bolivia.

6 Section Schufia

Central America and Mexico. Flowers are erect in terminal cymose panicles.

F. arborescens
Tube rosy purple, small.
Sepals rosy purple, small and narrow, reflexing.
Corolla lavender, small.
Foliage shiny green on top, paler green on the undersides. Leaves medium to large with reddish veins.
Growth shrubby upright to 25 ft (8 m). Flowers held erect in large panicles.
Mexico.

F. paniculata
Similar to *F. arborescens* except that the flowers are smaller and slightly darker in colour. Leaves are serrated.

7 Section Encliandra

Central America and Mexico. Flowers axillary, generally small and inconspicuous. Stamens short.

F. × bacillaris
Tube red, very small (5–6 mm).
Sepals rose, reflexing slightly.
Corolla rose, very small.
Foliage small, medium green and finely serrated.
Growth upright and bushy.
Mexico.

F. encliandra* ssp. *encliandra
(Syn. *F. encliandra.*)
Tube red, 6–8 mm long.
Sepals reddish, small.
Corolla reddish, flowers very small.
Foliage medium green, finely serrated, very small leaves.
Growth upright, bushy and fairly vigorous.
Mexico.

F. encliandra* ssp. *tetradactyla
(Syn. *F. tetradactyla.*)
Tube rose orchid to deep red, 7–10 mm.
Sepals red to scarlet.
Corolla rose scarlet or pale rose scarlet, small and compact.
Foliage dark green on top, lighter shade of green on the underside. Leaves small, serrated and pilose.
Growth shrubby, low growing. Young branches reddish.
Mexico and Guatemala.

F. microphylla* ssp. *hemsleyana
(Syn. *F. hemsleyana.*)
Tube rose pink, 5–7 mm long.
Sepals rose, slightly reflexed, small.
Corolla rose with a purplish tinge. Very small.
Foliage deep green on top, paler on the underside. Small and serrated.
Growth upright and bushy.
Panama and Costa Rica.

F. microphylla* ssp. *microphylla
(Syn. *F. microphylla.*)
Tube red, small.
Sepals deep red, small.
Corolla rose red, petals slightly serrated. Very small.
Foliage deep green on top, lighter green on the underside. Very small leaves.
Growth shrubby, upright.
Mexico.

F. microphylla* ssp. *minutiflora
(Syn. *F. minutiflora.*)
Tube reddish, 3–4 mm long.
Sepals reddish, small and held well out.
Corolla whitish, very small and compact.
Foliage deep green on top, paler on the undersides, very small and serrated.
Growth upright and shrubby.
Mexico.

F. parviflora
(Syn. *F. michoacanensis.*)
Tube red, 4–6 mm long.
Sepals red, slightly pilose, spreading.
Corolla coral red, very small.

Foliage darkish green, serrated and slightly pilose on the underside. Leaves very small.
Growth upright and shrubby with slender pilose branches.
Mexico, Guatemala and Costa Rica.

F. thymifolia* ssp. *minimiflora
(Syn. *F. minimiflora.*)
Tube whitish to reddish, less than 2 mm long.
Sepals whitish to reddish, small, reflexing.
Corolla white to red.
Foliage very small, medium green on top, paler on the underside.
Growth upright and bushy.
Mexico.

F. thymifolia* ssp. *thymifolia
(Syn. *F. thymifolia.*)
Tube white, reddening as it matures.
Sepals white, small and spreading.
Corolla white, becoming purplish-red as it matures.
Foliage medium green on top, lighter green on the underside. Very small.
Growth upright and shrubby. Young branches reddish and finely pilose.
Mexico.

8 Section Jimenezia

Costa Rica and Panama. Flowers in terminal racemes. Leaves opposite or in whorls.

F. jimenezia
Tube rose red to red, small.
Sepals rose red to red, short, wide and spreading.
Corolla rose pink, small.
Foliage dark green on top, paler green with a purple flush on the underside, slightly serrated. Leaves medium to large.
Growth climbing shrub to 6 ft (2 m). Flowers in terminal racemes.
Panama and Costa Rica.

9 Section Ellobium

Central America and Mexico. Leaves opposite and broad. Tubers generally present.

F. fulgens
Tube pink to dull scarlet, 60 mm long, narrow at the top becoming wider towards the base.
Sepals pale red, becoming greenish-yellow at the tips.
Corolla small, bright red.
Foliage sage green on top, lighter on the underside with a red flush. Large leaves, up to 7 in (17 cm), pilose and finely serrated.
Growth upright, shrubby with thickened tuberous roots. Flowers in racemes.
Mexico.

F. decidua
Tube reddish-pink, long and narrow, slightly constricted, pilose on the outside.
Sepals reddish-pink, small, held over the corolla.
Corolla red, very small.
Foliage medium green on top, lighter underneath, medium to large sized and pilose on the upper surface.
Growth epiphytic in trees or on rocks.
Mexico.

F. splendens
(Syn. *F. cordifolia.*)
Tube rose to bright red, medium to long, swollen then compressed at the base.
Sepals red at the base with green tips, short and spreading.

Corolla olive green, short.
Foliage medium green on top, lighter on the underside. Leaves medium sized, pilose, ovate to ovate-cordate.
Growth shrubby upright to 8 ft (2.5 m). Branches pilose. Axillary flowering.
Mexico to Costa Rica.

Cultivation of the species

Plants of many species can be grown in exactly the same way and under the same conditions as most of the hybrids and varieties, or cultivars as they are now known. In fact many of the fuchsias in Sections Quelusia and Encliandra can be hardy in all but the coldest areas.

However, the more commonly grown species, such as *corymbiflora*, *boliviana*, *fulgens*, etc., do require a very much more humid atmosphere if they are to do well, and also a freer root run, so they are happier in large pots of 25 cm (10 in) diameter or more. Few of these large species lend themselves to more than the minimum of shaping, preferring to grow naturally. Early feeding with a high nitrogenous fertilizer, changing in early summer to one with a high potash content, will produce large specimens in one or two seasons.

A minimum temperature of 4°C (40°F) should be sufficient to overwinter these large species.

For exhibition purposes the following are recommended:

F. arborescens
F. boliviana
F. boliviana luxurians
F. boliviana luxurians alba
F. denticulata
F. fulgens
F. fulgens 'Rubra Grandiflora'
F. fulgens var. *gesneriana*
F. magellanica var. *magellanica*
F. magellanica var. *macrostema*
F. magellanica var. *molinae*
F. paniculata
F. procumbens
F. regia var. *alpestris*
F. regia var. *regia*
F. splendens

and most of the Encliandra Section which are particularly good for small pot culture (see page 51).

There is much confusion in the naming of species and many of those grown today are incorrectly named. It is unlikely that *F. lycioides* is in general cultivation and it seems likely, therefore, that the plant so called by many growers is, in fact, a *F. magellanica* hybrid. Similarly, a large number of the Encliandra types currently available are either *F.* × *bacillaris* or seedlings. Plants of this type are very easily grown from seed.

Chapter 4
Hybridization

Hybridization is the production of new fuchsias by the means of deliberate crossing between two species, hybrids or cultivars, or any combination of these, using one as a seed parent and the other as the pollen parent with a view to producing fuchsias which are different to, and superior to, any already in existence. The difference need not necessarily be in colour, shape or form, but to be worthy of introduction into commerce nowadays, considering that over 6,000 fuchsias are already known to have been raised, and some 2,500 of these are presently available, any new fuchsia introduced should be something special. Unfortunately, the ease with which it is possible to grow fuchsias from seed has resulted in the appearance in recent years of a veritable glut of mediocre plants, few of which have been properly tested before release into commerce, and which then prove to be a great disappointment to anyone growing them. Sadly, these do not all come from amateur growers; many emanate from well-known hybridizers throughout Europe and elsewhere.

Before embarking on a programme of hybridization, one should ask oneself what the object is to be. It should be to try to combine the best characteristics of two fuchsias for bloom colour, foliage or

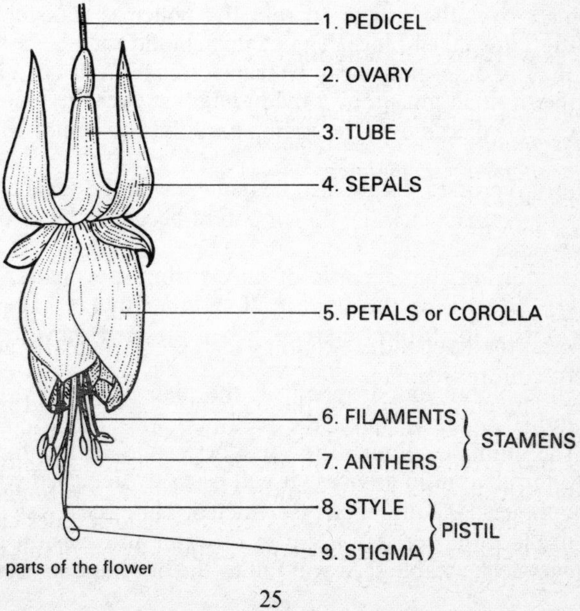

Fig. 4 The parts of the flower

type of growth; to breed in, by the use of suitable parents, new bloom colour combinations and/or growth habit, and generally to produce an improvement on anything already in existence. If these objects are pursued in the initial hybridization process, and a subsequent weeding out of any of the progeny which do not meet the required standard adhered to, then the number of new seedlings marketed will be greatly reduced and they might well be of a more lasting quality.

It might be of interest at this point to show the various parts of a fuchsia flower as hybridization infers an understanding of the functions of the various parts of the plant (Fig. 4). 1 The stalk, or pedicel. 2 The ovary which contains the ovules and, after fertilization, the seeds. 3 The tube, down which run the stamens and the pistil. 4 The sepals, or calyx. 5 The petals, or corolla. 6 The filaments. 7 The anthers, known together with the filaments as the stamens, on which pollen is produced. 8 The style. 9 The stigma, which, together with the style and ovary, forms the pistil, the female part of the flower.

Having chosen the two parent plants, one is designated as the seed parent and the other as the pollen parent.

Timing is critical as the pollen to be used must be completely fresh, and at the same time the seed parent must be at the stage where the stigma is receptive to the pollen, but before it has been liable to pollination from any other source. This condition can be attained by selecting, on the seed parent, a bud which is almost on the point of opening, then 'popping' it open gently between finger and thumb. Ease back the sepals and carefully remove the anthers and filaments. Then, taking a flower with ripe pollen from the pollen parent, brush the anthers over the stigma so that the pollen is transferred and fertilization has taken place. The stigma should then be covered to ensure that no other pollen can be transferred, and this can be done with either a small muslin or a nylon bag tied over the bloom, or a plastic capsule placed over the stigma until the flower dies and drops off.

Reciprocal crosses should also be made, using the same cultivars, but in a reverse role, i.e. the pollen parent becomes the seed parent and vice-versa.

It is important that records of all crossings are made, first by labelling each cross on the plant itself and then by keeping a record of every cross, for future reference when the seeds have been germinated.

Once the bloom has dropped off the plant, and provided that fertilization has taken place, the seed pod will start to swell and ripen. The ultimate colour of the ripe berry may be anything from green to purple, but in any case it will be easily detached when it is ripe and the seeds should then be extracted. The easiest way of doing this is to place the berry in a saucer of water and crush it between your fingers. The viable seed will fall to the bottom and the flesh of the berry, and any seed husks, will float. These can be removed and the seed on the bottom carefully tipped out onto a piece of blotting or kitchen paper.

Some berries may provide dozens of seeds while others may have only two or three. They should be dried out on the paper and stored carefully in an airtight container. It is often recommended that fuchsia seed should be sown when fresh, but it is better not to sow in autumn but to wait until the early part of the following year. Most fuchsias will flower in the first year from seed and there is little to be gained by sowing at a time when light levels and temperatures are very low.

Compost for seed sowing can be any proprietary seed compost, and seed trays, seed pans or pots are all equally suitable. The compost should be lightly firmed and watered, then left to drain before sowing the seed thinly on the surface. The seed should not be covered but just pressed gently into the compost. The tray is then covered over with a sheet of glass, or propagator top, and placed out of direct sunlight and preferably with some bottom heat to assist germination, which should take up to three weeks.

Seed sown in January or February should produce flowering plants by late summer although it may be necessary to keep some plants growing on over the following winter before they come into bloom.

When the young seedlings have made two pairs of leaves, they should be transplanted individually into small pots, no larger than 5 cm (2 in) in diameter, each clearly labelled with the crossing details, or otherwise marked so that the parentage is clear to the raiser. For this first potting, a good soil-less compost or John Innes No 1 is required, and no feeding other than that already incorporated in the compost will be necessary. Once the roots start to work their way into and through the compost, growth will be fast and the plants should be potted on whenever the roots start to fill the pot, moving up one size of pot at a time. Feed with a high nitrogen fertilizer to start with, then, when plants are put into a 12.5 cm (5 in) pot, change the fertilizer for one with a high potash content, to harden up the growth and encourage flower production.

During its first year the seedling plant receives little pinching out and shaping, the prime consideration being to bring it into flower for a preliminary assessment. It is at this stage that the grower has to start the 'weeding out' process, discarding any seedlings which do not come up to standard in that either the flower resembles something already in cultivation, or the growth is weak and perhaps susceptible to disease.

This process of elimination continues in subsequent years; in the second year the seedlings being grown as much for shape as for flower colour, until only the best remain. At least that is how it should happen in theory. Practice, unfortunately, tells a very different story. How can anyone justify a new seedling as 'an improved

Snowcap', for example? 'Snowcap', one of the best of the small red and white cultivars, is a must for every beginner to the art of growing fuchsias. It shapes itself and can be guaranteed to give masses of flowers with the minimum of care and attention. No fuchsia could be an improvement on 'Snowcap'!

Similarly, what can be expected of crosses using 'Royal Velvet' as either seed or pollen parent? Few hybridizers of today appear to know anything of the work of Gregor Mendel, or the meaning of dominant and recessive factors which he expounded in his *Laws of Inheritance*, published in 1865, and which, on re-publication in 1900, made possible a more scientific approach to plant breeding.

Back-crossing is seldom practised today, with the unfortunate result that there is a decided loss of vigour in many of the new cultivars being brought into cultivation. Continuous straight crossing and open pollination are leading to weaker and less stable plants, one of the reasons for the extraordinary number of so-called 'sports' which have appeared in recent years. Back-crossing is no mystery and is simply the process of crossing back a seedling with one or other of its parents in an attempt to introduce more of that parent's characteristics into the next generation of seedlings. This can be repeated numerous times until the right combination of desired characteristics is achieved.

Multiple crossing – trying to combine the best characteristics of three or more parents – is seldom practised, probably because of the time involved from the initial cross between the first two parents, the subsequent crossing of their offspring (F.1) with a third variety, or with the offspring of a second pair, and the eventual flowering and selection of plants from those seedlings. By this means a combination of genes from several parents can be obtained and the best qualities of all of them introduced.

However the crossings are done, the selection and weeding out of poor specimens are very important, and however difficult it may be for a grower to admit that a seedling may not be different, or an improvement on anything presently in cultivation, such seedlings *should* be destroyed. George Roe, who was a well-known hybridizer in Radcliffe on Trent for many years, grew, annually, up to 1,600 seedlings, of which rarely more than half a dozen were grown on for a second year – that is 'selection'.

Chapter 5

The Species Hybrids

From the very early days of commercial horticulture the introduction of new species of every genus, and the breeding of new hybrids from these species, have been very important. Look at any nursery catalogue today, or in any gardening publication, and you will see the attention and publicity given to novelties and new cultivars. Fuchsias are no different. From the time that previously unknown species were brought into Britain and Europe from the Americas, hybridizers were busy crossing and re-crossing in the hope of breeding something which would take the plant world by storm.

F. magellanica and *F. coccinea* were the first species to be grown in Europe in the last few years of the eighteenth century, closely followed by *F. lycioides*, *F. arborescens* and *F. fulgens*. Most of the early hybrids were crossed from *F. magellanica*, and, in fact, most of today's cultivars are probably descended from early *F. magellanica* × *F. fulgens* hybrids. 'Exoniensis' and 'Corallina', raised by Luccombe and Prince in 1843, were both from *F. magellanica* var. *globosa* × *F. cordifolia*. 'Dominyana', introduced in 1852 by Veitch of Exeter and raised by Dominy, was given as a *F. spectabilia* × *F. denticulata* seedling. In 1837, when *F. fulgens* and *F. corymbiflora* were introduced into England, a new era of fuchsia production started. The long tubes were at first a novelty, but the continuous use of these two species and their hybrids is evident in the number of such fuchsias still available today.

The work, done mainly in Germany, with *F. triphylla*, using *F. fulgens*, *F. splendens* and *F. cordifolia*, brought us what are now known as the Triphylla Hybrids and a large number of those early hybrids are not only still in cultivation, but are perhaps even more popular nowadays than they were in the early part of this century.

Use of the species in breeding gradually declined from the early 1900s and it was only in the 1970s that interest grew in them again, and then only with the Section Encliandra, with growers such as Jim Travis of Preston, and Henk van der Grijp, of Harfsen in the Netherlands, bringing out a number of interesting plants.

In the late 1970s and early 1980s, more species were being introduced into Europe from America, and a greater interest was being taken in correcting the mistakes in nomenclature which were the legacy left by Philip Munz in his *Revision of the Genus Fuchsia*. This was the first serious work on the fuchsia species, but in many cases identification was based solely on herbarium specimens and many incorrect identifications were made. The work of Dr Paul E. Berry,

Dr Peter H. Raven and Dennis Breedlove on the various sections of the genus has increased interest in the species and has corrected many of the previous errors in naming.

Herman de Graaff in Lisse, the Netherlands, and John Wright in Reading and then Lechlade, have done much work in breeding new hybrids, and although few of these can be said to have anything more than botanical interest, the doors are now re-opened for the breeding of different and more interesting cultivars. Breeding new fuchsias is not something which can be achieved in a few years, but we can, in the light of the more recent hybrids, look forward to some changes in the future, with new colours predominating. The yellow is still some way off, but it is not beyond the bounds of possibility that, out of the more recent crosses, that colour may yet be bred in to a greater extent than at present in some of the new species.

Cultivation

No blanket instructions for cultivating the species hybrids is possible because of the variation in the crosses being made, but it is safe to say that where *F. magellanica* is used the hybrid will be more or less hardy, and where *F. fulgens* and *F. triphylla* are used the cultivation details will be as found in the chapters on species and triphyllas. Encliandra crosses have the same habit as the type and will invariably need careful pinching to keep them in shape. They will require normal greenhouse conditions in winter and early spring.

A list of species hybrids

'Ariel'
TRAVIS 1970, *F. encliandra* × *F. hemsleyana*
Single
Tube magenta.
Sepals magenta with green tips.
Corolla deep pinkish-magenta.
Flowers very small.
Foliage deep green, breviflora type.
Growth small, upright.
Bush or mini standard.

'Bergnimf'
APPEL 1981, *F. sessilifolia* × *F. fulgens*
Single
Tube rose red, long and slender.
Sepals rose red, short.
Corolla red, short.
Foliage dark green.
Growth upright.

'Calumet'
DE GRAAFF 1985, (*F. fulgens* × *F. splendens*) × *F. triphylla*
Tube currant red.
Sepals currant red, reflexing at the tips.
Corolla mandarin red.
Foliage dark green with a reddish flush.
Growth trailer.
Basket or hanging pot.

F. colensoi
New Zealand
A naturally occurring hybrid between *F. perscandens* and *F. excorticata*. Similar in flower and other characteristics to *F. excorticata*.

'Diana Wright'
J. O. WRIGHT 1984, *F. magellanica alba* × *F. fulgens*
Tube flesh pink, long.
Sepals pink with green tips, long and reflexed.

Corolla phlox pink, small.
Foliage dark green with serrated edges.
Growth upright and bushy.

'Dominyana'
DOMINY 1852, *F. spectabilis* × *F. serratifolia*
Single
Tube, sepals and corolla scarlet.
Tube long and fairly thick.
Foliage dark purplish-bronze.
Growth upright.

'Fanfare'
REITER 1941, *F. denticulata* × *F. leptopoda*
Single
Tube scarlet, long.
Sepals scarlet, short.
Corolla turkey red.
Foliage darkish green.
Growth lax.

'First Success'
WEEDA 1983, *F. paniculata* × *F. splendens*
Single
Tube pink, small.
Sepals light pink.
Corolla opening lightish pink and maturing paler.
Blooms in clusters.
Foliage mid-green, large leaves.
Growth upright and vigorous.

'Grasmere'
TRAVIS 1964, *F. cordifolia* × *F. lycioides*? (More likely to have been the *F. magellanica* hybrid which is widely grown under the misnomer *F. lycioides*.)
Single
Tube and sepals coral red. Longish, thin tube.
Corolla coral pink.
Foliage deep green. Leaves largish.
Growth bushy upright.

'Highland Pipes'
DE GRAAFF 1983, *F. magdalenae* × *F. excorticata*
Single
Tube and sepals beetroot purple.
Corolla small, ruby red.
Foliage dark green with reddish veins. Paler on the underside of the leaves.
Growth lax upright, vigorous.

'Hinnerike'
BOGEMANN 1984, *F.* × *bacillaris* × *F. magdalenae*
Single
Tube darkish red, small and thick.
Sepals bright red, short and wide.
Corolla orange red, small and flaring.
Foliage dark green, small to medium sized leaves.
Growth small, upright and vigorous.

'Lady's Smock'
DE GRAAFF 1986 *(F. lycioides* × *F. magellanica)* × *F. paniculata*
Single
Tube and sepals rose magenta.
Corolla deep lilac ageing to lavender.
Foliage pale olive green with red veins. Paler on the underside of the leaves.
Growth upright, small and bushy.

'Lechlade Apache'
J. O. WRIGHT 1984, *F. simplicicaulis* × *F. boliviana*
Single
Tube red, long and thin.
Sepals red, short.
Corolla red, small.
Flowers in terminal racemes.
Foliage mid-green.
Growth upright and bushy.

'Lechlade Chinaman'
J. O. WRIGHT 1983, *F. splendens* × *F. procumbens*
Flowers small, amber-coloured.
Growth untidy.

'Lechlade Debutante'
J. O. WRIGHT 1984, *F. paniculata* × *F. lampadaria* (syn *F. madgalenae*)
Single
Tube long, pink.
Sepals pale pink with reflexing tips.
Corolla pink, small.
Foliage medium green on top, paler on the underside.

Growth upright, vigorous. Flowers held horizontally.

'Lechlade Fire Eater'

J. O. WRIGHT 1984, *F. triphylla* × *F. denticulata*

Single

Tube crimson, long and slender.

Sepals small, crimson with green tips and salmon on the underside.

Corolla orange.

Foliage dark olive green on the upper surface, reddish-purple on the underside.

Growth lax and untidy.

'Lechlade Gorgon'

J. O. WRIGHT 1985, *F. arborescens* × *F. paniculata*

Single

Flowers very similar to *F. arborescens.*

Growth very strong, difficult to control.

'Lechlade Maiden'

J. O. WRIGHT 1985 *(F. splendens* × *F. fulgens)* × *F. denticulata*

Single

Tube and sepals pink with green tips.

Corolla greenish-pink.

Foliage largish, mid-green.

Growth upright.

'Lechlade Potentate'

J. O. WRIGHT 1984, *F. splendens* × *F. lampadaria* (syn *F. magdalenae*)

Single

Tube brownish-red, long and slender.

Sepals red on top, salmon underneath, short.

Corolla salmon.

Foliage medium green.

Growth upright, vigorous and tall.

'Lechlade Rajah'

J. O. WRIGHT 1983, *F. boliviana* × *F. excorticata*

Single

Flowers long and purplish in colour.

Foliage darkish green.

Growth untidy.

'Lechlade Rocket'

J. O. WRIGHT 1984, *F. lampadaria* (syn *F. magdalenae*) × *F. fulgens*

Single

Tube pale orange red, long and thick.

Sepals orange red to green.

Corolla orange red.

Foliage dark sage green with reddish veins, paler on the underside.

Growth lax upright, untidy.

'Lechlade Tinkerbell'

J. O. WRIGHT 1983, *F. arborescens* × *F. thymifolia* ssp. *thymifolia*

Single

Encliandra type with small pink flowers.

Growth vigorous, upright.

'Lechlade Violet'

J. O. WRIGHT 1984, *F. paniculata* × *F. colensoi*

Single

Tube pale purple, olive green at the base, long and thin.

Sepals pale violet with green tips.

Corolla blackish-purple, small.

Foliage pale green, lighter on the underside.

Growth upright, very vigorous.

'Lunters Zon'

APPEL 1987, *F. fulgens* × *F. boliviana*

Single

Tube orange, long and thin.

Sepals orange.

Corolla orange, small.

Flowers in terminal racemes.

Foliage large, medium green.

Growth upright, vigorous.

'Maori Pipes'

DE GRAAFF 1985, *F. excorticata* × *F. triphylla*

Single

Tube and sepals rose magenta.

Corolla bright red, small.

Foliage dark green, paler green on the underside.

Growth upright and vigorous.

'Mary'

BONSTEDT 1894, *F. triphylla* × *F. corymbiflora*

Single

Flowers long, bright scarlet.

Foliage dark sage green.
Growth upright and bushy.

'Mayella'
VAN DER POST 1987, *F. magdalenae* × *F. pilaloensis*
Single
Tube rose, long and thin.
Sepals rose on top, pale coral on the underside.
Corolla orange-red to bright orange.
Foliage dark green, paler underneath.
Growth lax, upright.

'Miep Aalhuizen'
DE GRAAFF 1987, *F. arborescens* × *F. venusta*
Single
Tube magenta, long and narrow.
Sepals pinkish magenta.
Corolla opens pink and ages to dark pink.
Foliage light yellowish-green.
Growth upright and vigorous.

'Northumbrian Pipes'
DE GRAAFF 1983, *F. arborescens* × *F. magdalenae*
Single
Tube china rose, long and narrow.
Sepals lavender pink, recurving.
Corolla light lavender pink.
Foliage fuchsia green.
Growth lax upright.

'Oos'
VAN DER GRIJP 1973, *F. parviflora* × *F. microphylla*
Flowers and foliage breviflora type.
Blooms red, small.
Growth upright and bushy.

'Oosje'
VAN DER GRIJP 1973, *F. parviflora* × *F. microphylla*
Flowers red, small.
Foliage mid-green, small.
Growth upright and bushy. Breviflora type.

'Pink Cornet'
J. O. WRIGHT 1981, *F. boliviana* 'Alba' × *F. boliviana forma puberulenta*
Single
Tube pink, long.
Sepals white and slender.
Corolla red. Flowers small.
Foliage large, mid-green.
Growth upright, bushy.

'Pink Trumpet'
J. O. WRIGHT 1981, *F. boliviana* × *F. boliviana* var. *luxurians*
Single
Tube long, pink.
Sepals white, slender.
Corolla bright red.
Foliage green, large leaves.
Growth upright, vigorous.

'Red Rain'
DE GRAAFF 1986 (*F. lycioides* × *F. magellanica)* × *F. triphylla*
Single
Tube and sepals dark red.
Corolla dark red, small.
Foliage light yellowish-green with reddish veins.
Growth upright, small and bushy.

'Rina Felix'
WESTEINDE-FELIX 1984, *F. fulgens* var. *Gesneriana* × *F. colensoi*
Single
Tube neyron rose.
Sepals neyron rose at the base, then pale greyish-yellow changing to scheele's green.
Corolla dark reddish-purple.
Foliage mid-green.
Growth small, upright.

'Small Pipes'
DE GRAAFF 1985, *F. paniculata* × *F. triphylla*
Single
Tube and sepals dark magenta.
Corolla dark mallow purple.
Blooms like *F. paniculata.*
Foliage dark green.
Growth upright, vigorous.

'Space Shuttle'
DE GRAAFF 1981 *(F. splendens* × *F. fulgens)* × *F. splendens*
Single
Tube and sepals red.
Corolla red with some yellow on the petals.

Foliage medium green.
Growth upright.

'Twiggy'

DE GRAAFF 1980, *F. magellanica* × *F. lycioides*
Single
Tube neyron rose, long and thin.
Sepals rhodonite red, long and slender.
Corolla lilac mauve.
Foliage fuchsia green.
Growth trailer, lax and untidy.

'Uillean Pipes'

DE GRAAFF 1986, *F. paniculata* × *F. sanctae-rosea*
Single
Tube and sepals magenta.
Corolla light rose pink.
Blooms in panicles.
Foliage dark green.
Growth lax, upright.

'Vincent van Gogh'

VAN DER POST 1979, 'Speciosa' *(F. splendens* × *F. fulgens)* × *F. fulgens* 'Rubra Grandiflora'
Single
Tube pale lilac red.
Sepals pale rose with green tips.
Corolla light rosy purple.
Foliage medium green.
Growth trailer.

'Whiteknight's Amethyst'

J. O. WRIGHT 1980, *F. magellanica* × *F. excorticata*
Single
Tube reddish-purple.
Sepals pale reddish-purple, yellowish-green at the tip.
Corolla violet, maturing to reddish-purple.
Foliage dark green, small leaves.
Growth upright, vigorous.

'Whiteknight's Cheeky'

J. O. WRIGHT 1980, 'Whiteknight's Ruby' *(F. triphylla* × *F. procumbens)* × *F. procumbens*
Single
Tube dark tyrian purple, long triphylla type.
Sepals dark tyrian purple.
Corolla dark tyrian purple. Flowers small, in terminal racemes.
Foliage dark green with red veins.
Growth upright, bushy.

'Whiteknight's Pearl'

J. O. WRIGHT 1980, *F. magellanica* var. *molinae* × *(F. magellanica* var. *molinae* × *F. fulgens)*
Single
Tube white, small and thin.
Sepals pale pink.
Corolla pink.
Foliage dark green, small.
Growth upright and bushy.

'Whiteknight's Ruby'

J. O. WRIGHT 1976, *F. triphylla* × *F. procumbens*
Single
Tube red to purple, long.
Sepals small, tyrian purple.
Corolla tyrian purple, small.
Foliage dark green with red veins.
Growth upright and bushy.

Chapter 6

The Triphylla Hybrids

The triphylla hybrids are descended from *F. triphylla* and are recognised by their flowering habit, which is in terminal racemes. The flowers are mainly in shades of red and orange, although recent introductions include salmon pink and one which is almost white, with just slight traces of pink on the sepals. Foliage in the triphylla hybrids is usually darkish, shiny green with red or purplish-bronzing on either or both leaf surfaces.

F. triphylla was the first fuchsia known to horticulture, having been discovered by Père Plumier in Santo Domingo at the end of the seventeenth century, although it was not known in Britain until nearly a hundred years later, when Henderson of St John's Wood sent a plant to Kew for identification.

There is some confusion as to which was the first triphylla hybrid to be introduced and credit is usually given to 'Thalia', said to have been introduced by Turner in 1855. However, Turner's 'Thalia' was a white-tubed cross from 'Venus Victrix' and had no triphylla blood in it. The 'Thalia' grown today, a known triphylla hybrid, is attributed to the German raiser Bonstedt.

Despite the fact that *F. triphylla* was grown in Britain from the 1880s, no use seems to have been made of it in hybridizing, and it was the Germans, particularly Rehnelt and Bonstedt, who pursued this avenue with great success. In the early part of the twentieth century they produced between them such excellent hybrids as 'Andenken an Heinrich Henkel' (1902), 'Traudschen Bonstedt', 'Göttingen' and 'Thalia' in 1905, and 'Koralle' and 'Gartenmeister Bonstedt' in 1906. An earlier hybrid from Bonstedt was 'Mary' in 1894, said to be a cross between *F. triphylla* and *F. boliviana*, and probably the first of the triphylla hybrids. Its scarlet flowers and greyish green foliage make it one of the most attractive hybrids remaining from those early crossings.

Little work then appears to have been done for almost four decades, until Victor Reiter in America produced 'Trumpeter' from a 'Gartenmeister Bonstedt' cross and then, two years later, in 1948, 'Mantilla'.

In Britain 1966 saw the introduction of 'Billy Green', a chance seedling given to Bernard Rawlins, a nurseryman in London, which was to be a great favourite with exhibitors at shows in Britain for many years. The same seedling was found at Wreste Park College in Bedfordshire and grown as 'Wreste Park' for some years, but whether it has any *F. triphylla* blood in it is a matter for conjecture.

Suffice it to say it looks very much a 'triphylla type'.

Harry Dunnett from East Anglia brought out several new triphylla hybrids in the 1970s, including 'Stella Ann' and 'Timlin Brened', and Edwin Goulding of Ipswich has also produced a number, not the least of these being 'Our Ted' which is almost pure white. In 1976 Karl Nutzinger in Austria introduced 'Elfriede Ott' from a cross between 'Koralle' and *F. splendens*, a salmon pink double of slightly lax habit, but nevertheless a beautiful plant.

Growers in many countries are using *F. triphylla* and its hybrids in their crossings at present, but, with the exception of 'Our Ted' (Goulding 1986), there are few with any outstanding features.

Cultivation

The triphylla hybrids are not difficult to cultivate if some cardinal rules are adhered to. They will not tolerate too much water, and waterlogging of a plant in a pot will soon result in the roots rotting and the plant dying. They are not frost-hardy, and in winter must have temperatures of not less than 4°C (40°F) and no more than 10°C (50°F). Like some of the species, they do not appreciate the same amount of pinching out as ordinary cultivars, and two or three early pinches will be sufficient to form a well-shaped plant. Most triphylla hybrids tend not to break from the base in spring, resulting in a bare expanse of wood at the bottom of the plant.

Recommended triphylla hybrids and triphylla types

'Andenken an Heinrich Henkel'
'Baker's Tri'
'Billy Green'
'Gartenmeister Bonstedt'
'Koralle'
'Mantilla'
'Mary'
'Our Ted'
'Stella Ann'
'Thalia'
'Traudschen Bonstedt'
'Trumpeter'

Chapter 7

Composts and Fertilizers

In normal gardening parlance the word 'compost' refers to decayed organic matter, such as grass cuttings, vegetable stalks, prunings, etc., which is stored in such a way that it rots down over a period and can then be returned to the garden. When dug in, as humus, it will enrich the soil.

In recent years, however, compost has also come to mean the medium in which seeds are sown, cuttings rooted and in which pot plants are grown and it is in that context that the word is used here.

Innumerable proprietary brands of compost are available to the grower nowadays, and these can be split into three types: soil-based, peat-based and soil-less. Each has its devotees, but the main function of a good compost is that it should be able to produce a strong, healthy root system to support and nurture the plant. A free-draining structure is also essential, but not so free-draining that it dries out quickly. A certain amount of moisture retention is needed to keep the plant healthy.

Some composts contain nutrients, but their efficiency may be only short-lived, especially as they can be quickly leached out by watering. Regardless of the compost used, liquid feeding has to be done as a matter of routine.

John Innes composts

These are made up to formulae worked out over 50 years ago at the John Innes Institute, and are based on a constant ratio of:

7 parts by volume of medium loam
3 parts peat
2 parts sand

to which is added a quantity of John Innes Base fertilizer, which is made up of:

2 parts, by weight, of hoof and horn
2 parts superphosphate of lime
1 part of sulphate of potash

The various compost formulae are then made up as follows:

John Innes Seed Compost

To each bushel is added 43 g (1 oz) of superphosphate of lime and 21 g ($\frac{3}{4}$ oz) of ground chalk.

John Innes No 1
Add 113 g (4 oz) of JI Base fertilizer and 21 g ($\frac{3}{4}$ oz) of ground chalk per bushel.

John Innes No 2
Add 227 g (8 oz) of JI Base fertilizer and 21 g ($\frac{3}{4}$ oz) of ground chalk per bushel.

John Innes No 3
Add 340 g (12 oz) of JI Base fertilizer and 21 g ($\frac{3}{4}$ oz) of ground chalk per bushel.

Much of the commercially available John Innes Compost has the JI Base already mixed in, and this has been found to cause toxicity if stored for a long time. It is better to look for composts where the JI base is packed separately for mixing when the compost is ready for use.

When used with fuchsias the John Innes No 1 is suitable for cuttings; No 2 for the first potting, and No 3 for later potting and baskets.

Soil-less composts

These were introduced some 25 years ago, following research by the University of California, and consisted of a mixture of moss peat and sand in various proportions. Like most innovations in horticulture, this one created numerous initial problems, the main one being difficulty in watering, but nowadays soil-less composts are commonplace and most of the early difficulties have been ironed out. Points in their favour are that they are light, clean and very easy to use, although from experience I would suggest that they are only suitable for plastic pots, and that where a grower uses clay pots, a soil-based compost is more efficient.

The amount of fertilizer incorporated in proprietary composts is rarely stated on the container and, as for soil-based composts, a regular feeding programme must be adhered to.

Peat-based composts

These are more or less the same as soil-less composts, but there is always a preponderance of peat with very little sand or grit. With both types it is always advisable to add a good quantity of grit or sharp sand, to ensure that there is good drainage.

Good quality moss peat is widely available and many growers make up their own compost. They can thus control their growing techniques better, knowing exactly what the compost incorporates and thus being able to judge when and how much water and feeding will be required.

Good coarse grit or sand is often difficult to obtain, but a suitable soil-less compost can be made up as follows:

80% fine moss peat

20% sharp sand or grit

with the addition of a proprietary fertilizer mix for soil-less composts, e.g. Chempak soil-less fertilizer mixture.

Horticultural perlite is freely available and this, too, can be incorporated into compost to improve drainage. It should, however, be dampened before it is used.

One important fact which must be taken into account is the pH level of the compost in which fuchsias are grown, the ideal being between 6.5 and 7. Higher or lower pH levels could he harmful to the plant and might also inhibit the availability of nutrients.

Feeding and fertilizers

For healthy growth plants need nutrition, and where they are grown in pots that nutrition has to be given in the form of either solid or liquid fertilizers.

The main nutrients are nitrogen, potassium, phosphorus and calcium.

Nitrogen is responsible for the healthy growth of the shoots and foliage, but should not be used to excess as the resultant growth will be soft and more prone to disease.

Potassium encourages stronger, harder growth and promotes flower production and colour.

Phosphorus is essential for root development.

The role of *calcium* is in the formation of cell tissues.

Each of these has a part to play in the development of the plant and most general fertilizers include them in different ratios.

However, on their own they are insufficient to ensure healthy growth, and a number of other elements should also be given to the plants in lesser quantities. These include:

Magnesium, active in the production of chlorophyll. A deficiency will cause chlorosis.

Iron, also necessary for the production of chlorophyll.

Boron, which the plant needs in order to take up calcium.

Very small amounts of these elements are required and most are available in liquid form.

Chapter 8

Training Fuchsias

Training a fuchsia into one of the many recognised forms should start immediately it is into its first pot from the rooted cutting stage. However, the choice of suitable cultivars for each type of growth is of great importance, and a list of recommended cultivars is given for each type of growth, and fully described, on page 79 *et seq*. The most common types of growth are the bush and the shrub, and these are similar in all respects except that the bush is grown on a short single stem of no more than 4 cm ($1\frac{1}{2}$ in) and the shrub has multiple growths from below soil level.

As from 1988, the British Fuchsia Society's *Judges and Exhibitors' Handbook* no longer uses the definition of a shrub, but permits the exhibition of this type of plant in classes for bush fuchsias. Although the shrub is no longer a separate 'trained type' for show purposes, there are many cultivars which lend themselves better to this manner of cultivation than to the short single stem method, hence the description and list of recommended cultivars given below.

Bush

Once the cutting is into its first small pot, the growing tip should be removed after a maximum of three pairs of leaves have formed. This will encourage the formation of sideshoots and the basic growth framework. These sideshoots should have their tips removed after two or three pairs of leaves, and this process continues until the required size and shape are achieved.

Whether the pinching out of the growing tips is done after two or three pairs of leaves have been formed depends largely on the vigour of the cultivars being used. Some fuchsias have long internodes, i.e.

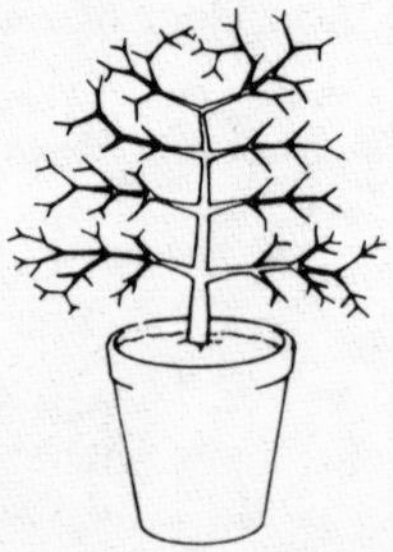

Fig. 5 Bush

a long length of stem growth between the nodes or leaf joints, and it is these which should be stopped at two pairs of leaves to avoid producing a tall, open plant structure. Those with shorter internodes, stopped at every third pair of leaves, will make a more compact and considerably denser plant. There are growers who stop at every pair of leaves, but this tends to make the plant too tight, and invariably leads to the foliage and flowers being much smaller than normal, giving the plant a very stunted look.

Stopping (the pinching out of the growing tips) will delay flowering, and, as a general rule, eight to ten weeks should be allowed between the last stop and flowering for single-flowered cultivars, and between ten and fourteen weeks for double-flowered cultivars.

Once the final stop has been given, the plant will continue to grow, but provided the job has been done regularly and methodically over the whole plant each time, the end result should be a framework which, when viewed from any angle, is entirely symmetrical. If the pinching out has been haphazard, growth will be uneven and flowering could be delayed and patchy.

Shrub

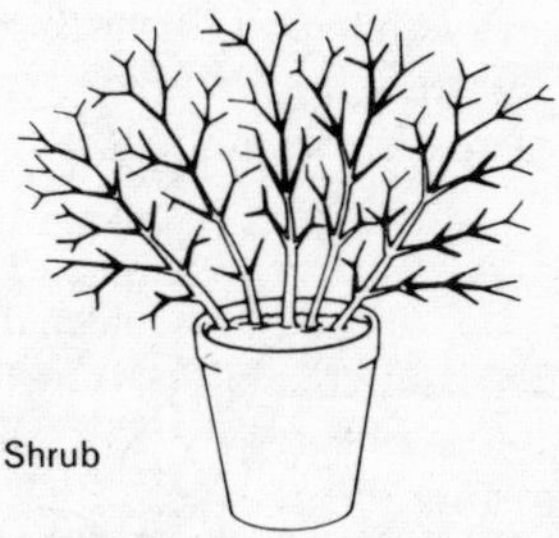

Fig. 6 Shrub

The type of cutting best used to produce a shrub plant is one which is short-jointed and has a good strong root system. It should be potted fractionally deeper than usual, so that the first set of nodes is beneath the soil level. These will produce shoots, and, when the pinching out process is followed, growth from the base will thicken up and numerous shoots will be produced from under the soil. Growing tips are removed in exactly the same way as for the bush plant and the final shape should be the same.

Recommended cultivars for bush and shrub culture

'Abbé Farges'
'Achievement'
'Aintree'
'Alan Ayckbourn'
'Albion'
'Alf Thornley'
'Alison Ewart'
'Alison Reynolds'
'Amanda Jones'
'Amy Lye'
'Angela Leslie'
'Annabel'
'Army Nurse'
'Athela'
'Bambini'
'Barbara'
'Beacon'
'Beacon Rosa'

'Bealings'
'Bicentennial'
'Billy Green'
'Blowick'
'Blue Elf'
'Blue Gown'
'Blue Waves'
'Blush of Dawn'
'Bobby Shaftoe'
'Bobby Wingrove'
'Bon Accorde'
'Border Queen'
'Bountiful'
'Bow Bells'
'Brutus'
'Burning Bush'
'Caledonia'
'Cambridge Louie'
'Camelot'
'Cardinal Farges'
'Carl Wallace'
'Carlisle Bells'
'Carmel Blue'
'Carmen Maria'
'Carol Roe'
'Caroline'
'Celia Smedley'
'Charming'
'Chartwell'
'Checkerboard'
'Cheviot Princess'
'Chillerton Beauty'
'Christmas Elf'
'Citation'
'City of Leicester'
'Cliff's Unique'
'Clipper'
'Cloth of Gold'
'Cloverdale Jewel'
'Cloverdale Pearl'
'Cloverdale Pride'
'Cloverdale Star'
'Coachman'
'Collingwood'
'Come Dancing'
'Constance'
'Coquet Bell'
'Coquet Dale'
'Countess of Aberdeen'
'Countess of Maritza'
'Cropwell Butler'
'Dalton'
'Dark Eyes'
'Derby Imp'
'Display'
'Doctor Brendan Freeman'
'Dollar Princess'
'Donna May'
'Doreen Redfern'
'Dorothea Flower'
'Dr Topinard'
'Dulcie Elizabeth'
'Dusky Beauty'
'Eden Lady'
'Edith Emery'
'Edna May'
'Eleanor Clark'
'Eleanor Leytham'
'Emile de Wildeman' (syn. 'Fascination')
'Estelle Marie'
'Eva Boerg'
'Evensong'
'Fiona'
'First Kiss'
'Flirtation Waltz'
'Florence Mary Abbott'
'Flying Scotsman'
'Forward Look'
'Garden News'
'General Monk'
'Genii'
'Glenby'
'Glororum'
'Golden Border Queen'
'Golden Eden Lady'
'Golden Treasure'
'Graf Witte'
'Heidi Ann'
'Heidi Weiss'
'Herald'
'Hidcote Beauty'
'Iceberg'
'Icecap'
'Iced Champagne'
'Impudence'
'Indian Maid'
'Isle of Mull'
'Jean Ewart'
'Joan Pacey'
'Joy Patmore'
'Kegworth Beauty'
'Kegworth Supreme'
'Ken Jennings'
'Kerry Ann'
'Keystone'
'Khada'
'King's Ransom'
'Kolding Pearl'
'Lady Isobel Barnett'
'Lady Kathleen Spence'
'Lady Patricia Mountbatten'

'Lady Ramsey'
'Lady Thumb'
'Lakeland Princess'
'Lancelot'
'Lena Dalton'
'Leonora'
'Leonora Rose'
'Liebriez'
'Lilac Lustre'
'Linda Goulding'
'Lindisfarne'
'Little Jewel'
'Lochinver'
'Loeky'
'Lord Roberts'
'Loveliness'
'Lustre'
'Lye's Unique'
'Madame Cornelissen'
'Margaret Pilkington'
'Margaret Roe'
'Margaret Rose'
'Marin Glow'
'Maureen Munro'
'Mauve Beauty'
'Max Jaffa'
'Mayfield'
'Mazda'
'Micky Goult'
'Mieke Meursing'
'Minirose'
'Mipam'
'Miss California'
'Mission Bells'
'Molesworth'
'Monsieur Thibault'
'Mr A. Huggett'
'Mrs Lawrence Lyon'
'Mrs Lovell Swisher'
'Mrs Marshall'
'Mrs Popple'
'Nancy Lou'
'Norman Mitchinson'
'Northway'
'Oriental Lace'
'Other Fellow'
'Pacquesa'
'Papoose'
'Party Frock'
'Patricia Ewart'
'Paul Roe'
'Paula Jane'
'Pearl Farmer'
'Pennine'
'Peppermint Stick'
'Perky Pink'
'Perry Park'
'Pink Bon Accorde'
'Pink Darling'
'Pink Fairy'
'Pink Pearl'
'Pirbright'
'Pixie'
'Playford'
'Plenty'
'Pop Whitlock'
'President Leo Boullemier'
'Preston Guild'
'Prince Syray'
'Prosperity'
'R.A.F.'
'Ravensbarrow'
'Ridestar'
'Robbie'
'Rolla'
'Ron Ewart'
'Rose of Castile'
'Rose of Castile' improved
'Rose of Denmark'
'Rosecroft Beauty'
'Royal Purple'
'Royal Velvet'
'Roy Walker'
'Rufus'
'Sandboy'
'Santa Barbara'
'Saturnus'
'Scarcity'
'Siobhan'
'Snowcap'
'Sonata'
'Son of Thumb'
'Southgate'
'Spion Kop'
'Strawberry Delight'
'Swanley Gem'
'Taddle'
'Tennessee Waltz'
'Thalia'
'Tom Thumb'
'Tom West'
'Troika'
'Tsjiep'
'Unique'
'Upward Look'
'Viva Ireland'
'Vivienne Thompson'
'Waveney Waltz'
'Wendy Leedham'
'White Pixie'
'Winston Churchill'
'W. P. Wood'

Standard

There are four types of standard: the mini standard, with a length of clear stem, between 15 and 25 cm (6–10 in) from soil level to the first branch; the quarter or table standard, between 25 and 45 cm (10–18 in); the half standard between 45 and 75 cm (18–30 in); and the full standard, between 75 and 105 cm (30–42 in). The training pattern for each is the same.

The cultivar chosen should be one which has a strong upright habit of growth as this, especially for the beginner, makes the job much easier and the standard reaches maturity a great deal quicker than if a less vigorous cultivar is used.

There are a number of fuchsias, better known as trailing or basket types, which will make very showy weeping standards, but these do tend to take longer to grow up to the required height.

A worthwhile hint when choosing a cutting to grow on into a standard plant is to look for one where the leaves are in sets of three rather than in pairs. By using such a cultivar there will be a 50% increase in the number of sideshoots formed and an equivalent increase in the number of flowers. Some cultivars habitually produce three-leaved shoots, e.g. 'Snowcap' and 'Rufus', both vigorous plants.

From the time the cutting is first potted it should be supported and loosely tied to its stake. A young plant will need no more than a thin split cane. This can be changed to a more substantial cane as the plant grows, always ensuring that the ties are not so tight as to cut into the stem. This support is necessary to produce a straight stem on the standard.

As soon as they are large enough to handle without damaging the

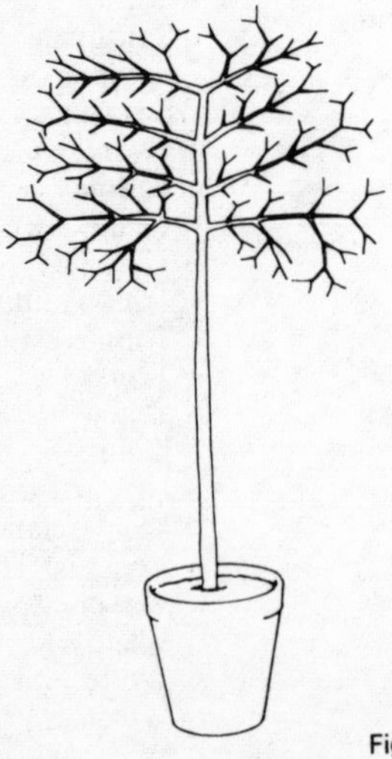

Fig. 7 Standard

plant the side shoots should be removed, but the main leaves on the stem are left in place as it is through these that the plant lives and breathes. The growing tip is also left intact until the plant has reached the height required. Removal of the sideshoots encourages the upward growth of the plant as all of the plant's energy is concentrated in the growing tip.

The finished standard should be in the proportion of one-third head to two-thirds stem, and it is this formula which decides when the pinching out of the sideshoots should finish and when the tip should be removed. For example, if the desired height of the standard is 75 cm (30 in), 50 cm (20 in) should be the stem length and 25 cm (10 in) the depth of the head, so, when the total growth has reached 50 cm (20 in), the sideshoots should be left in place from there on, and when the overall height has reached 75 cm (30 in), the growing tip is removed. The formation of the head of the standard is then done in the same manner as for a bush or shrub, the side-shoots, resulting from the removal of the growing tip being stopped at every three pairs of leaves until a head proportionate to the stem has formed.

Recommended cultivars for use as full or half standards

'Aintree'
'Amy Lye'
'Ann H. Tripp'
'Annabel'
'Athela'
'Barbara'
'Billy Green'
'Bon Accorde'
'Border Queen'
'Brilliant'
'Brutus'
'Cambridge Louie'
'Cardinal'
'Carlisle Bells'
'Carmen Maria'
'Celia Smedley'
'Chang'
'Charming'
'Checkerboard'
'City of Leicester'
'Clipper'
'Cloverdale Pearl'
'Constance'
'Coquet Bell'
'Coquet Dale'
'Countess of Maritza'
'Display'
'Doctor Brendan Freeman'
'Doreen Redfern'
'Dorothea Flower'
'Eden Lady'
'Edith Emery'
'Emile de Wildeman' (syn. 'Fascination')
'Estelle Marie'
'Eva Boerg'
'Fiona'
'Flying Scotsman'
'Glororum'
'Golden Border Queen'
'Golden Eden Lady'
'Herald'
'Iceberg'
'Icecap'
'Isle of Mull'
'Jack Acland'
'Joan Pacey'
'Joy Patmore'
'Kegworth Beauty'
'Kegworth Supreme'
'King's Ransom'
'Lady Isobel Barnett'
'Lakeland Princess'
'Leonora'
'Lilac Lustre'
'Lindisfarne'
'Little Jewel'
'Lochinver'
'Lord Roberts'
'Loveliness'
'Lustre'
'Lye's Unique'

'Margaret Pilkington'
'Margaret Roe'
'Margaret Rose'
'Mauve Beauty'
'Mayfield'
'Mazda'
'Melody'
'Micky Goult'
'Mieke Meursing'
'Mipam'
'Miss California'
'Mission Bells'
'Monsieur Thibault'
'Moonlight Sonata'
'Mrs Lovell Swisher'
'Mrs Marshall'
'Mrs Popple'
'Nancy Lou'
'Norman Mitchinson'
'Northway'
'Other Fellow'
'Pacquesa'
'Party Frock'
'Patricia Ewart'
'Pearl Farmer'
'Pennine'
'Perry Park'
'Petronella'
'Phyllis'
'Pink Pearl'
'President Leo Boullemier'
'Preston Guild'
'Prince Syray'
'Prosperity'
'Ravensbarrow'
'Ridestar'
'Rolla'
'Rose of Castile'
'Rose of Castile' improved
'Royal Purple'
'Rufus'
'Scarcity'
'Siobhan'
'Snowcap'
'Taddle'
'Tennessee Waltz'
'Ting a Ling'
'Upward Look'
'Waveney Waltz'
'Wendy Leedham'
'White Pixie'

Recommended cultivars for use as quarter or mini standards

'Abbé Farges'
'Alan Ayckbourn'
'Alison Ewart'
'Alison Reynolds'
'Amanda Jones'
'Amy Lye'
'Bealings'
'Bobby Wingrove'
'Cardinal Farges'
'Carol Roe'
'Cliff's Unique'
'Cloverdale Pride'
'Countess of Aberdeen'
'Cropwell Butler'
'Derby Imp'
'Dollar Princess'
'Donna May'
'Dr Topinard'
'Dusky Beauty'
'Eden Lady'
'Edna May'
'Eleanor Clark'
'Eleanor Leytham'
'Excalibur'
'Flirtation Waltz'
'Florence Mary Abbott'
'Glenby'
'Heidi Ann'
'Heidi Weiss'
'Hidcote Beauty'
'Jean Ewart'
'Ken Jennings'
'Kerry Ann'
'Khada'
'Lady Ramsey'
'Lady Thumb'
'Lancelot'
'Lena Dalton'
'Liebriez'
'Linda Goulding'
'Loeky'
'Madame Cornelissen'
'Marin Glow'
'Maureen Munro'
'Minirose'
'Mr A. Huggett'
'Mrs Lawrence Lyon'
'Oriental Lace'
'Papoose'
'Paul Roe'
'Paula Jane'
'Peppermint Stick'
'Pink Bon Accorde'
'Pink Darling'
'Pink Fairy'
'Pirbright'
'Playford'
'Plenty'

'Pop Whitlock'
'Robbie'
'Ron Ewart'
'Rosecroft Beauty'
'Roy Walker'
'Sandboy'
'Santa Barbara'
'Son of Thumb'
'Tom Thumb'
'Tsjiep'
'Unique'
'Vivienne Thompson'
'Winston Churchill'

Basket

Suspended just above head height, with masses of bloom cascading down over the edges of the basket, this is probably one of the most attractive ways of growing fuchsias, and there are numerous cultivars well suited to this type of growth.

Nowadays there are many different types of hanging basket: the traditional plastic-covered wire baskets; solid plastic baskets with a built-in saucer to prevent drying out in summer; square cedarwood baskets with brass chains, in fact a basket to suit every purpose and situation. Even the problem of how to line the basket would seem to have been solved with the introduction of fibre basket liners. However, the best way of lining a basket is still to use sphagnum moss, and this is widely available at garden centres for those unable to collect it in the wild.

For ease of handling sit the basket on top of a bucket, then fill it with a lining of well-damped moss to a thickness of about 2.5 cm (1 in) around the edges, pressing it firmly against the sides so that it covers the wire framework. The compost can then be added gradually, taking care not to disturb the lining too much, and firming it slightly as you go along. In a normal 37.5 cm (15 in) basket, five plants should be sufficient, but the only golden rule which applies to hanging baskets is that all the plants should be of the same variety.

The ideal size of plant to use is one from a 9 cm (3 in) pot, as, at this size, it should have a good amount of both top and root growth. Four plants are placed equidistant from one another around the edge of the basket, the compost filled in around them and gently firmed, and a shallow depression left in the middle. The basket should then be watered and left to drain. It is better to leave the

Fig. 8 Basket

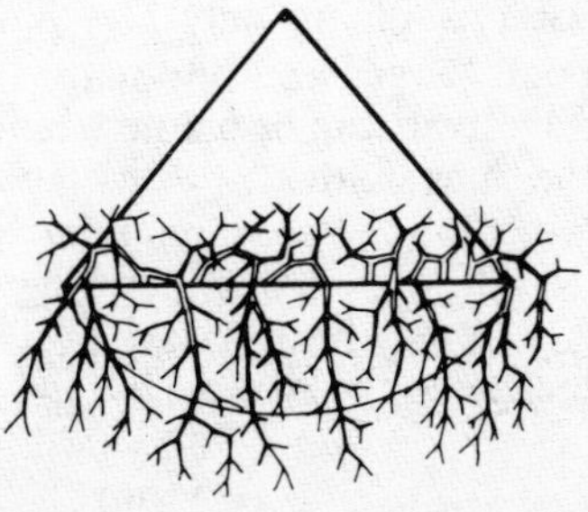

basket on top of the bucket for a couple of weeks or so until the plants are established, before hanging it in the greenhouse. After a week or so the fifth plant can be placed in the centre of the basket. Having spent this extra time in its pot, without a check, it will have made more upright growth, which will soon fill out the centre of the basket, giving it height rather than an overall flat top.

Pinching out of the growing tips will encourage further growth to fill out the basket before the plants start to trail over the edges and cascade downwards.

Planting a half basket is very similar to a basket, but three plants are sufficient.

Recommended basket and half basket plants

'Anna of Longleat'
'Auntie Jinks'
'Balkonkönigin'
'Bicentennial'
'Blue Veil'
'Blush of Dawn'
'Carnival'
'Cascade'
'Clifton Beauty'
'Crackerjack'
'Curtain Call'
'Daisy Bell'
'Derby Imp'
'Eva Boerg'
'Frank Unsworth'
'Frome in Bloom'
'Frosted Flame'
'Golden Anniversary'
'Golden Marinka'
'Ian Leedham'
'Jack Shahan'
'Joy Bielby'
'Karen Bielby'
'Kegworth Carnival'
'La Campanella'
'Lakeside'
'Mantilla'
'Marinka'
'Molesworth'
'Orange Mirage'
'Pinch Me'
'Pink Galore'
'Pink Marshmallow'
'Postiljon'
'President Margaret Slater'
'President Stanley Wilson'
'Princessita'
'Red Spider'
'Rose of Denmark'
'Sophisticated Lady'
'Swingtime'
'Taffeta Bow'
'Trailing Queen'
'Trail Blazer'
'Troika'
'Vanessa Jackson'

Hanging pots

One would grow the same type of fuchsia in a hanging pot as in a basket, but one or two plants only are used in a 16 cm ($6\frac{1}{2}$ in) diameter hanging pot. Larger sizes of pot are available and in these, two, three or more cultivars can be planted, but, as for baskets, these should all be of the same cultivar.

The cultivation method is the same as for baskets, pinching out the growing tips to fill the pot, then allowing the plant to cascade down over the edges. It may be necessary to remove more tips from the branches to thicken up the growth, but this depends a lot on the cultivars chosen.

Recommended cultivars for hanging pots

All of the basket cultivars, and also:
'Alwin'
'Bobby Shaftoe'
'Coachman'
'Come Dancing'
'First Kiss'
'Golden Arrow'
'Iced Champagne'
'Margaret Pilkington'
'Max Jaffa'
'Moonlight Sonata'
'R.A.F.'

Pyramid and conical

The cutting is grown on until it has made five pairs of leaves, then the growing tip is removed. This will encourage the growth of the sideshoots. Of the top pair of sideshoots, the weaker should be pinched out. The remaining shoot is tied in to a stake and, again, after four or five pairs of leaves have been formed, the tip is removed and the weaker of the resultant topmost sideshoots taken out. This procedure is repeated until the required height is reached. At the same time as this process is being followed, normal pinching out of the other sideshoots is done to keep the plant in shape.

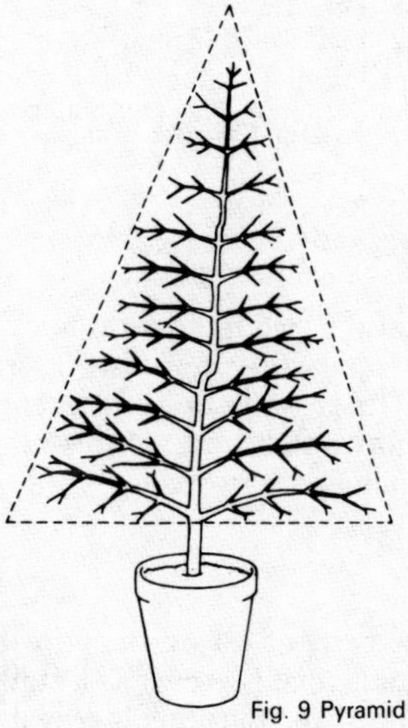

Fig. 9 Pyramid

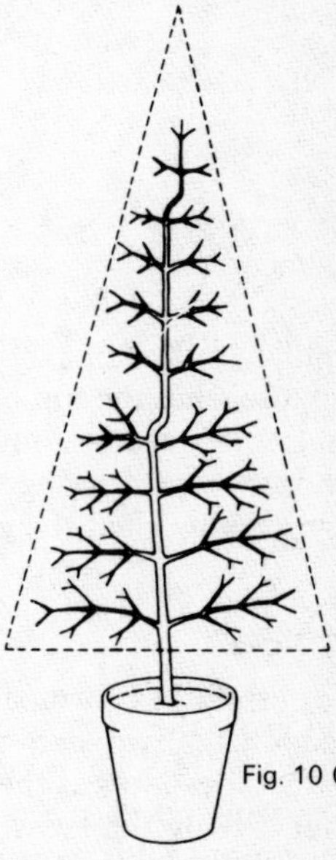

Fig. 10 Conical

Fan

When the cutting has made five pairs of leaves, the growing tip is removed and the resulting sideshoots tied in to a fan-shaped frame-

Fig. 11 Fan

work. After each of these sideshoots has made a further five pairs of leaves the tips are again taken out, and this pinching-out and tying-in process continues until the framework is completely clothed.

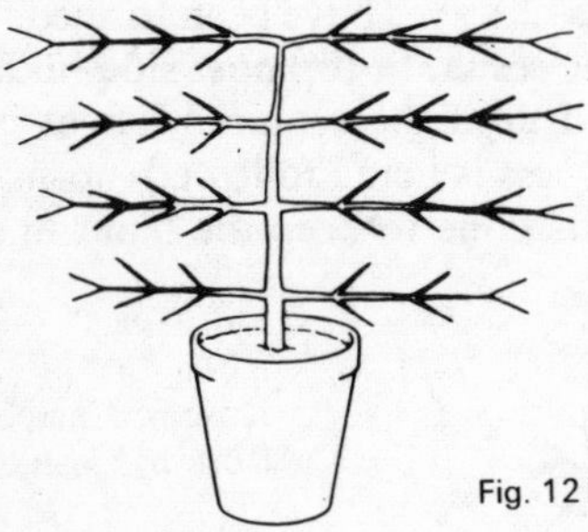

Fig. 12 Espalier

Espalier

This is similar to the fan except that the leading shoot is allowed to grow until it reaches the top of the framework previously inserted in the pot in a series of horizontals. The growing tip is then removed, the sideshoots trained along the horizontals and the tips removed when they have reached the extremities.

Pillar

When the cutting has formed three pairs of leaves, the growing tip is removed. Of the two leading shoots, one is grown as a standard, removing the sideshoots as they appear, and the other is grown as for a bush, but leaving the growing tip on until the shoot reaches half the height of the finished plant. The resulting sideshoots on this growth are then pinched out as for bush culture, while the first shoot, being grown as a standard, is allowed to grow until it reaches the desired height, when the tip is removed and culture from there on is the same as for a standard. The idea is that the part treated as a standard will clothe the top half of the plant, and that treated as a bush the bottom part.

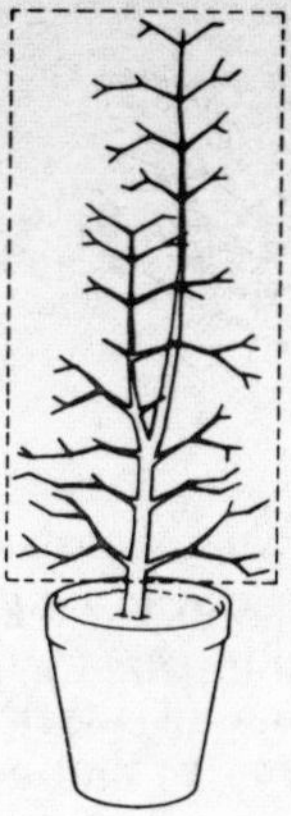

Fig. 13 Pillar

Recommended cultivars for pyramid, conical, fan, pillar and espalier culture

'Barbara'
'Brilliant'
'Brutus'
'Cardinal'
'Checkerboard'
'Constance'
'Display'
'Edith Emery'
'Mrs Lovell Swisher'
'Phyllis'
'Pink Pearl'
'Rolla'
'Rose of Castile'
'Rose of Castile' improved

Small pot culture

This method of growing fans, espaliers, etc., is becoming very popular. The maximum size of pot which can be used is one of 13 cm ($5\frac{1}{4}$ in) diameter, and great care must be taken to use only those cultivars which are proportionate to the pot. Most of today's fuchsias do not lend themselves well to small pot culture and only the Encliandra types are really suitable. Cultivation is exactly the same as for the normal growth types.

Chapter 9

Growing for Exhibition

There are two methods of growing fuchsias – the annual method in which cuttings taken early in the year are grown to maturity in one season; and the biennial method where cuttings are taken in June or July, grown on to, say, an 11 cm (4½ in) pot by the end of the first season, overwintered at 7°C (45°F) and grown to maturity in the following season.

The Annual Method

Cuttings are struck as early in the year as possible and when heat is available in the greenhouse. If they are propagated with heat from below, from a heated propagator or soil-warming cables, they should root in two weeks or so, and are then potted up into a small pot of 5 cm (2 in) diameter. They should be kept in a draught-free atmosphere for a few days, until they have settled down after the shock of removal from the propagator, and shaded from direct sunlight.

If the cuttings are to be grown as bush or shrub plants the growing tip should be removed at the earliest possible moment after potting up. Those selected for standard growth should have the growing tip left intact. Even at this early stage a small split cane should be inserted for support.

Feeding, with a high-nitrogen liquid fertilizer, should start when the cuttings have been potted for about two weeks, and this should be continued weekly. Growth will be fast as the plants settle in to the new compost and it is essential that they are potted on as soon as the roots start to fill the pot. They must never be allowed to become pot-bound at this early stage. Potting up should be gradual, in stages of one pot size at a time, from 5 cm (2 in) to 7.5 cm (3 in), then to 10 cm (4 in) and so on. The plants should be into their final 16 cm (6½ in) pots by the end of June or early July.

In the middle of the season, when the plants are almost into their final pots, the feeding programme should be changed to a high potash fertilizer to encourage hardening of the wood and the production of blooms.

Plants should be turned in the greenhouse at least twice every week in order that they do not grow one-sided, particularly if the greenhouse does not receive full light all day long. It may be necessary to shade the greenhouse during long hot spells, to stop the plants drying out or becoming scorched. This can be done with closeweave plastic netting or by painting the glass with one of the proprietary brands of shading paint.

The importance of watering cannot be overstressed. Plants should never be allowed to dry out as this could stop their development, and when the weather is particularly hot it is advantageous to soak the floor and staging, to keep the humidity levels up and prevent wilting.

Biennial method

This method is mainly used for the production of exhibition bush and shrub plants, and cuttings are taken and rooted in late June or early July. They are potted up as necessary and trained to the desired shape by the removal of the growing tips as normal, but they will not be potted into larger than 11 cm (4½ in) pots during that first year.

As autumn approaches, the amount of water given is slightly reduced to encourage the plants to slow down their growth. They should be kept in a temperature no higher than 4°C (40°F) over the winter period. In late January or early February heat is increased to 7°C (45°F) and the plants restarted into growth. It may be necessary to prune slightly to remove any unwanted branches, but the basic framework of the plants, which was built up in the previous season, should be retained. As the plants grow they are fed with a liquid high-nitrogen fertilizer and potted up whenever the roots are filling the pots, changing the feeding to one of high potash in mid-season. As with plants grown on the annual system, the optimum size of pot in the first year should be 16 cm (6½ in).

Potting back

In spring those plants which flowered the previous year and which have been overwintered in the greenhouse, or elsewhere, will need to be potted back. This comprises knocking a plant out of its old pot, removing as much of the spent compost and dead roots as possible, then repotting it in fresh compost in a smaller sized pot. This will encourage the production of new roots, and when the plant starts into growth, it should be pruned back to one or two nodes from each joint.

Blooms

Exhibiting in blooms classes is becoming very popular, particularly with those exhibitors who may not have sufficient plants of show quality but can always pick a number of good flowers.

The flowers should be in first-class condition, completely fresh and without any sort of blemish or sign of pests or disease. The flowers should be of the normal size for the variety, not immature. Pollen is permitted on the anthers, but should not be visible elsewhere on the flower.

Chapter 10

Fuchsias in the Home, in Tubs and in Windowboxes

Few fuchsias will grow well indoors, the main reason for this being that the atmosphere of modern centrally heated homes is too dry for a plant which needs humidity to give of its best. It is, however, sometimes possible to create reasonable growing conditions by plunging the pot into a larger container of gravel, which is kept moist, and by regularly mist-spraying the foliage. Older plants which are already well budded or in flower, will soon drop their blooms indoors, and it is perhaps better to start off with cuttings which will adapt better to the drier conditions. These can generally be flowered successfully, provided that light conditions are also good.

Larger plants may be brought into the house for short spells of up to three days, but they must then be returned to the greenhouse or patio.

Windowboxes and tubs

Plants to be used in windowboxes should come from pots no smaller than 9 cm ($3\frac{1}{2}$ in), and planted out when any danger of frost is over. The type of compost used in the windowbox may be of any type, John Innes or soil-less, and the cultivars chosen from those which do not grow too tall as they would then look very much out of place. An eventual height of 15–30 cm (6–12 in) is all that is required. Distance between plants in a windowbox should be the same as the height of the plants, and a maximum of four plants is recommended. After planting out, the plants should be treated as if they were still in pots, fed and watered regularly, and sprayed as usual against pests and diseases. They should be taken out of the container before they are touched by frost and stored in a frost-free environment.

Growing in tubs is very similar to growing in a windowbox, except that the cultivars are of a different type – it is very effective to plant a tall variety in the centre of the tub, or a quarter standard, filling in the outside with dwarf upright varieties or trailing cultivars.

Chapter 11

Fuchsias as Summer Bedders

As summer bedding plants, fuchsias can be used to fill any available garden space, and are guaranteed to give a brilliant show of colour during the summer and early autumn months. Little soil preparation is needed other than to ensure that there is free drainage. Once the ground has been dug over and prepared, a light dressing of a general fertilizer, or bonemeal, can be raked in.

Some forward planning should be done before planting to take account of flower and foliage colour and plant height so that the finished article will be pleasing to the eye as well as allowing every plant to be seen to its best advantage. For example, if the bed can be viewed from all sides, the dwarf or low-growing varieties should be placed round the outside edge, building up in height to the tallest plant or plants in the centre. As central or 'dot' plants, it is best to use quarter or half standards, well staked to avoid damage by wind.

As well as planting to accommodate plants of different heights, colour must be taken into account to give the bed a balanced appearance. There are a number of small varieties with variegated foliage, which look well as edging plants, and it might be worth while alternating these round the edge with other dwarf plants with brightly coloured flowers. To draw the eye farther into the bed, some plants of the cultivar 'Genii', with its bright yellow foliage, will contrast nicely with other green-leaved fuchsias, and the triphylla 'Thalia', with its orange scarlet flowers and dark bronzy foliage, is also an excellent and showy plant for summer bedding.

Where flower colour is concerned, try not to plant fuchsias of the same variety, or with similar flower colour, too close to one another. There is practically no limit to the number of fuchsias which can be used for summer bedding, so a great selection of colours is available. The list on page 79 *et seq.* gives some ideas which may be of help in planning a border.

Planting out fuchsias for summer bedding is best left until the end of May or early June, depending on the area in which you live and the likelihood of late frosts. Plants should not be too small, ideally from 12.5 cm (5 in) pots and upwards, although the dwarf edging plants could come from 9 cm ($3\frac{1}{2}$ in) pots. I would recommend that plants are taken out of their pots, experience having shown that plants bedded out in pots tend to dry out very quickly during hot dry spells. Also, roots do grow out through the bottom and over the tops of the pots, making it difficult to remove them when they have to be lifted later in the season.

They must be lifted before they are cut down by frost – this could be any time from late September onwards – and overwintered as in Chapter 15.

During the growing season they should be watered regularly, fed weekly with a liquid fertilizer and sprayed against possible attack by pests or disease.

Chapter 12

Garden Hardies – Fuchsias as Permanent Bedding Plants

A large number of fuchsias are listed by nurserymen as hardies, but as field trials for hardy fuchsias have been very few in number, such listings must be treated with caution. Wisley Gardens in Surrey have held hardy trials on several occasions, but while winters there can be severe, they can hardly be compared with conditions in more northerly areas. In recent years a number of 'hardy' fuchsias have emanated from the Isles of Scilly where I would doubt that frost is ever experienced, but they are said to have been bred from recognised hardy cultivars and that in itself must give them some chance of survival.

However, it must be said that, while there is no fuchsia which is guaranteed to survive very severe winters, there are enough to make the creation of a permanent fuchsia border worth while if attention is paid to the selection of suitable varieties and the planting is properly done.

First, the situation of the border. It should not be north-facing, nor should it be in full shade from trees, buildings, etc. A slightly dappled shade, to take off the full glare of the sun, might be an advantage as plants would not dry out so quickly, but full shade would cause plants to become drawn and weak.

The soil should be neither too heavy nor too light; a medium free-draining loam is best. It is always worth checking the pH of the soil to ensure that it is not too acid or alkaline, with an ideal pH of about 6.5 to 7.

Planting time will be any point from late May to mid-June, as soon as any danger of frost is past. The planting holes should be dug half as deep again as the depth of the pot from which the plant is taken and 1 oz of bonemeal should be incorporated into the bottom. Plants from 4½ in pots or larger should be used. The extra depth at which they are planted will mean that perhaps half of the top growth is then under the surface, but this affords much more protection from frost than they would have if planted at their own depth. Water them in well and ensure that they do not dry out during their first season. Feed regularly with a liquid fertilizer and spray against pests and diseases. In future years a light dressing of general fertilizer, raked in around the plants, will be sufficient, but spraying of insecticides and fungicides should be routine.

Pruning of the old wood should be left until the spring as it does help to protect the plants during winter frosts.

A hardy fuchsia bed will give a great deal of colour for five months of the year, from June until October, but to extend the beauty of such a bed to 12 months, it is a good idea to intersperse the fuchsias with various types of heathers, ericas and callunas. These are available in great variety and can be particularly colourful during the autumn, winter and early spring months, with their golden, silver and dark green foliage, and blooms ranging from white to deep red and purple. Like hardy fuchsias, they need little attention once they are established.

'Alison Reynolds'

Cuttings in a pot with rooting compost

The same pot, the cuttings rooted

A well-rooted cutting

Plate in a 6-cm (2½ in) pot, ready for its first stop

The same plant stopped

Fuchsias growing in a rockery

Cuckoo spit

The froghopper, the cause of cuckoo spit

Damage by thrips

Vine weevil larvae

Adult vine weevil

Whitefly

Whitefly

Fuchsia rust

'Ron Ewart'

'Jean Ewart'

'Lye's Unique'

F. splendens

'Pacquesa'

'Vivienne Thompson'

'Impudence'

'Dalton'

F. *boliviana alba*

'Stanley Cash'

'Genii'

'Mary'

'Bon Bon'

Basket display

'Swanley Yellow' half baskets

'Bon Bon'

Wall baskets in a Dutch garden

'Khada'

'Marinka'

Chapter 13

Fuchsia Hedges

It is as a hedge that the fuchsia really comes into its own as a garden plant. Grown naturally, with the minimum of attention, it can provide a summer-long blaze of colour.

Fuchsia hedges are an integral part of the landscape in south-west England, the coastal areas of south-west Ireland, and on the Antrim coast of Northern Ireland, particularly on the route between Cushendall and Cushendun, where the roadsides are a mass of colour from the end of June through to the end of September.

How they came to be planted there can only be a matter for conjecture as many of these hedges, judging by the thickness of the basal wood, must be many decades old. It is a tradition, however, amongst Irish Quakers, that fuchsia hedges were planted by their forbears following the potato famine of the 1800s, the original plants being brought from Brittany.

The success or otherwise of a fuchsia hedge is largely dependent on the area in which one lives, the varieties chosen for the purpose and the care with which the ground is prepared for planting. Area is important as, although the cultivars one would use to make a hedge would be winter-hardy, the season, as one goes north, is progressively shorter and the likelihood of the hedge ever fulfilling its purpose is much less. A fuchsia described in a nursery catalogue as 'hardy' could well prove disappointing, but there are numerous good hedging fuchsias including the *F. magellanica* hybrids and these are listed on page 79.

Planting a fuchsia hedge, like any other permanent garden feature, requires considerable forethought and planning. The first question one must ask is, 'What type of hedge do I want?' There are basically two types – the traditional hedge growing to 1 m (4 ft) or more in height, which can be trimmed to shape each summer, and that of 90 cm (3 ft) or less, which is more of a divider between two parts of the garden than a proper hedge. Whichever one chooses will determine the cultivars to be used, although the ground preparation is the same in either case.

Soil preparation

The soil condition is important as fuchsias will not grow in just any garden soil. It must be free-draining and at the same time not prone to drying out in spells of hot weather.

A heavy clay soil tends to compact in wet weather, hindering the passage of air to the roots, while in hot weather it dries into solid lumps, with the same effect. A considerable amount of humus should be added to counteract this. Garden compost, leaf mould, chopped straw or bracken, or spent mushroom compost are all ideal additives, which, when incorporated in quantity, will open up the soil structure to make it less water-retentive.

The initial rough digging over of the area on this type of soil should be done in the autumn, allowing the winter frosts to start breaking down the lumps. In early spring it should be dug over again and the compost, etc., added.

Light soils are less of a problem, but quite often these are too free-draining and, here again, the addition in the spring of some humus – leaf mould, well-rotted manure or garden compost – is advantageous. Deep digging is unnecessary, two spits being sufficient.

Planting

The time of planting must necessarily vary according to the area and the likelihood of late frosts. This can be from early May to the end of June, but, in any case, it is helpful if some cloche protection is given after planting to ensure that the young plants do not suffer an early setback.

The plants should always be pot grown to ensure a good root system, without which they would struggle for existence when planted out in the open. The optimum size is from a 12.5 cm (5 in) pot; not too small as to have a poor root system and not so large that it is old and potbound.

The distance between the plants is of some importance as the final hedge should be continuous and without gaps, but it is difficult to be too precise as the eventual growth and height are largely dependent on area and weather conditions. However, as a rule of thumb, where the given height of the plants is 76 cm ($2\frac{1}{2}$ ft) or less, the distance apart should be 30 cm (12 in), and where it is 76 cm ($2\frac{1}{2}$ ft) or more, planting at 45 cm (18 in) apart should suffice.

The planting hole should be dug to a depth 50% greater than the depth of the pot from which the plant is taken, and 57 g (2 oz) of bonemeal should be incorporated into the bottom inch. This extra depth will afford added protection to the roots in winter as, when the plant is placed in the hole, perhaps half its original top growth will be under soil level. Replace the soil carefully around the plant and gently firm it in, leaving a slight depression round the top for watering, so that the water will go directly to the roots. Plants should be watered straight away after planting to help them recover from any check.

For the remainder of their first year after planting the plants should be treated in the same way as if they were still in pots, i.e. watered and fed regularly and sprayed against pests and diseases.

Although hedging plants should have made good growth by the time the first of the winter frosts arrive, it is always advisable to give them some extra protection by covering the crowns with peat, sand or straw.

Pruning back should not be begun until spring when the new growth has started from the base. The old wood is then pruned back to two buds from the base. In milder areas, growth often restarts all the way along the old wood, and in these areas pruning back is unnecessary, although a light trimming out of weak and misshapen growths can be done.

In early spring a light dressing of a good general fertilizer should be raked in around the hedge. This done, no further attention should be necessary other than routine spraying of insecticides and fungicides, or watering in any prolonged hot, dry spells until the hedge is well established.

Chapter 14

Ornamental and Variegated Fuchsias

These form a very interesting part of the genus, ranging, as they do, from bright yellow to reddish foliage in the ornamentals, through silver, golden yellow, white, pink and red in the variegateds. All variegated fuchsias may be held to be ornamental, but the strict definition of each type is that ornamental-leaved cultivars are those with foliage of one colour only, excluding green, while variegated-leaved cultivars have foliage of more than one colour, one of which may be green.

The great majority of ornamental- and variegated-leaved fuchsias are, in fact, sports or mutations from ordinary green-leaved cultivars and species, and many, particularly the newer introductions, have a tendency to revert from time to time to their original foliage colour.

Foliage colour is, to a great extent, influenced by growing conditions. For instance, the cultivar 'Genii', when grown outdoors in a sunny aspect, will have bright yellow leaves, while in the less bright or shaded atmosphere of the greenhouse, it is liable to produce leaves of medium green.

The uses to which ornamental- and variegated-leaved fuchsias may be put are many. They are just as adaptable as any other fuchsia in this respect and will do well in ordinary pot culture, hanging baskets, wall baskets or hanging pots, in tubs and windowboxes, as summer bedding plants and as hedging plants.

There are only two areas where their culture differs slightly, first in watering, as some cultivars, particularly those with pale or yellow leaves, do tend to be more prone to botrytis than other fuchsias, and also in the feeding programme where it is essential that phosphates are given in sufficient quantity to preserve and accentuate the foliage colour and strength.

Where ornamental- and variegated-foliage plants are grown for exhibition, it is on their foliage and shape alone that they are judged, the flowers generally being of little importance (the exceptions being in the basket and hanging pot classes).

The following lists are of cultivars recommended for the various types of growth.

Pot Culture

Ornamental-leaved fuchsias	*Foliage colour*
'Barry's Queen'	bright yellow
'Genii'	bright yellow
'Golden Border Queen'	bright yellow

'Golden Eden Lady'	bright yellow
'Golden Wedding'	bright yellow
'Gold Leaf'	lemon yellow
'Graf Witte'	greenish-yellow
'Morning Light'	lettuce green
'Pixie'	yellowish-green
'President'	reddish-green
'Strawberry Delight'	bronzy yellow
'White Pixie'	yellowish-green

Variegated foliage

F. m. magellanica aurea	gold and green
'Cloth of Gold'	yellowish-bronze
'Golden Cloverdale Pearl'	gold and green
'Golden Runner'	gold and green
'Golden Treasure'	gold and green
'Green 'n' Gold'	yellow and cream
'Herbe de Jacques'	red and gold
'Old Somerset'	green, pink, mottled
'Ornamental Pearl'	grey green and cream
'Pop Whitlock'	grey green and cream
'Potney's Tricolor'	green, white and cream, tinged red
'Rosecroft Beauty'	pale green with golden-yellow edges, shaded cream and cerise
'Sharpitor'	cream and pale green
'Sunray'	green, creamy white and cerise
'Tom West'	cream, pale green, silvery and reddish
'Wave of Life'	greenish-gold

Hanging Baskets and Half or Wall Baskets

Ornamental-leaved fuchsias

'Daisy Bell'	reddish-green
'Golden Swingtime'	golden yellow

Variegated foliage

'Golden La Campanella'	green and gold
'Golden Lena'	green and gold
'Golden Marinka'	green and gold
'Tom West'	reddish-silver

Hanging Pots

Ornamental-leaved fuchsias

'Daisy Bell'	reddish-green
'Golden Swingtime'	golden yellow

Variegated foliage

'Autumnale'	copper red and gold
'Golden La Campanella'	green and gold
'Tom West'	green, cream and reddish-silver

Tubs and Windowboxes

Plants in these will fare best if grown in a sunny aspect, although not in direct sunlight all day, which could damage the foliage, especially if pale coloured. Quarter standards may be used as 'dot' plants in tubs, smaller bush plants being placed round the edge. In windowboxes the ultimate height of plants should be no more than 30 cm (12 in).

Ornamental-leaved fuchsias

'Coquet Gold'	lemon green
'Genii'	golden yellow
'Gold Leaf'	lemon yellow
'Golden Border Queen'	golden yellow
'Golden Eden Lady'	bright yellow
'Graf Witte'	greenish-yellow
'Morning Light'	lettuce green
'Pixie'	yellowish-green
'President'	reddish-green
'Strawberry Delight'	reddish-green
'White Pixie'	yellowish-green

Variegated foliage

'Cloth of Gold'	yellowish-bronze
'Golden Cloverdale Pearl'	green and gold
'Golden Runner'	green and gold
'Golden Tolling Bell'	pale green/yellow
'Golden Treasure'	green and gold
'Green 'n' Gold'	yellow and cream
'Herbe de Jacques'	red and gold
'Old Somerset'	green, pink, mottled
'Ornamental Pearl'	grey green and cream
'Pop Whitlock'	grey green and cream
'Potney's Tricolor'	green, white and cream, tinged red
'Rosecroft Beauty'	pale green with golden yellow edges, shaded cream and cerise
'Sharpitor'	cream and pale green
'Sunray'	green, creamy white and cerise
'Tom West'	cream, pale green, silvery and reddish

Summer Bedding

All of the cultivars listed above under tubs and windowboxes can be used. Ornamental- and variegated-foliage cultivars are best used as 'dot' plants, or edging plants, to provide a contrast with the ordinary green-leaved plants.

Hedging Plants

None of the ornamental-leaved fuchsias are really suitable for use as hedging plants as their ultimate height is rarely more than 61 cm (2 ft), but there are a few variegated-leaved cultivars which will attain 90 cm (3 ft) or more. These are best used in conjunction with green-leaved cultivars, planting one variegated- to every two green-leaved plants. The variegation is then more noticeable.

The two best plants for this purpose are:

F. magellanica macrostema variegata	green and silver
F. 'Tricolori'	cream, green and pink

Chapter 15
Overwintering Fuchsias

The overwintering of fuchsias creates a problem for many people, and it is true that most losses do occur during the winter. However, it is more often careless storage that is to blame for this than actual exposure to frost, and perhaps the biggest single reason for fuchsias dying in winter is that they have been kept dry. Even although they are in a dormant state, they still require a minimum of moisture to keep them alive, for, once dried out, the roots shrivel and die with the result that the plant itself dies.

It is often assumed by gardening writers, when talking about winter care of plants, that everyone has a heated greenhouse, or at least a greenhouse which can be kept free of frost. This is seldom the case, and so for most gardeners keeping their fuchsias over the winter can be a problem. Where the fuchsias are permanently planted in the ground, i.e. hardy varieties planted at the correct depth (see page 57), they will survive all but the most severe of winters, but it is the fuchsia grown in a pot that requires special treatment.

For the gardener without glass the easiest method of winter storage is in a trench in a sheltered corner of the garden, and this should be prepared before the onset of frost. Naturally, the size of the trench depends on the number of fuchsias to be stored in it, but a trench of 90 × 61 and 90 cm in depth (3 × 2 × 3 ft) will safely accommodate 30 to 40 plants. The only other requirements are a quantity of slightly damp, but not wet, peat and a small amount of straw or bracken to act as a lining for the bottom and sides. The soil dug out of the trench should be removed for use elsewhere as it is unlikely to be of any use for this purpose.

The fuchsias to be put in the trench for storage should be cut back by about one-third of their height, and completely defoliated. This is easily done by running the branches up between thumb and forefinger to remove the leaves, which, if left on, would rot and cause botrytis. The compost in the pots should then be dampened, not soaked.

A layer of straw or bracken is put in the bottom of the trench, then an inch or two of moist peat and, finally, the plants are laid on their sides in whichever manner they best fit, head to head, or head against the next pot. As the trench is filled, more peat should be added to filter down amongst the plants and straw, or bracken placed against the sides to about 15 cm (6 in) from the top. No plants should be placed nearer the surface than this in case of severe frost. The trench should be levelled out with more peat and its position marked by a cane at each corner. For extra protection, the top of the trench may be covered with plastic sacking or any other material which will not rot.

The plants can remain safely in the trench until the beginning of April when they are carefully removed. Most will be found to have started into growth. As they have been devoid of light, the new growths will be white and perhaps long and spindly, but once in the light again they will soon green up and may be used as cuttings taking them back to the first joint from the main stem each time. New growth will soon be of the normal kind and the plants can be pinched out in the usual manner. Remember, however, that they will still require protection from frost, at least until the end of May, before being put out of doors.

The alternative to the trench method, for those who do not have a greenhouse, is storage in some other frost-free environment – a shed or garage for example, or in an insulated attic or loft. I hesitate to suggest the use of a spare bedroom, but if this is the only place available then so be it. Just as in the trench method, the plants should be trimmed back by one-third, defoliated and slightly dampened. They can then be rolled, in their pots, in old newspaper and packed into cardbroad boxes for storage. Polystyrene boxes, if available, give added protection as they do have more insulation. The advantage of plants stored in this manner is that they can be inspected regularly to ensure that they are not drying out. They are removed from their boxes in the same way and at the same time as trenched plants.

A cold frame may also be used for overwintering. If the frame is lined with polystyrene sheeting, and the plants buried in the soil in their pots, then covered over with peat, they should be perfectly safe. Some ventilation should be given from time to time so that the plants do not damp off, and where severe weather is forecast, sacking may be placed over the frame lights to give a little added protection.

Overwintering in the greenhouse is less of a problem. In a cold greenhouse, one with no heating of any sort, insulation would be of some help. Perhaps the best type of insulation one can use is the 'bubble plastic' sheeting, which is available in several widths for the amateur's greenhouse. There are special fittings for use in aluminium greenhouses, but whichever type of greenhouse you have, it must be remembered that to have any effect, there should be a gap of 2.5–4 cm (1–$1\frac{1}{2}$ in) between the sheeting and the outer glass. Claims that the use of this material can make a difference of 5 degrees or more between the inside and outside temperatures in winter make it certainly worth a try. As an additional safeguard, plants can be dug into the soil underneath the bench and covered over with peat, straw or old newspapers – anything to give that little extra protection.

The heated greenhouse affords the fuchsia grower the ideal method of overwintering, but as – with the exception of those being grown by the biennial method (see page 53) – fuchsias should ideally be in a dormant state over the winter period, the temperature should be kept as low as possible, preferably no more than 1.6–3.3°C (35–38°F) until February when it can be raised to 4–7°C (40–45°F) to start the plants into growth again.

Chapter 16

Pests and Diseases – Recognition and Control

Fuchsias are no more susceptible to attacks by pests and diseases than any other plant, and with the tremendous range of insecticides and fungicides available nowadays, it should be possible to keep them completely clean and healthy.

Pests and diseases rarely attack plants which are grown in clean surroundings and it is therefore of prime importance that good hygiene is practised in the greenhouse. Fallen leaves should be removed from pots, staging and floor areas, plants with symptoms of pest or disease attack should be put into a quarantine area outside the greenhouse, and any new plants should also be kept separate for a few days, to allow any infection which they might be carrying to manifest itself. Additionally, during the winter months the greenhouse should be scrubbed down with disinfectant to remove any overwintering eggs or spores which may be concealed on the glass or staging.

Common pests

Aphids

These are mainly greenfly and blackfly, although the latter rarely attack fuchsias. The eggs are usually laid on the undersides of the leaves and these hatch out into immature females, called nymphs. As they grow, they shed their skins and eventually become wingless adults capable of producing live young. Winged females are also produced and they will move to other plants, lay eggs and continue the cycle.

Aphids suck the sap from the plants and are mainly found on young leaves and shoots, causing distortion of the foliage and buds. The honeydew which they produce attracts a sooty mould which is very unsightly and disfiguring.

Control of aphids is achieved by spraying with a contact or systemic insecticide, the latter being preferable as any aphids sucking the sap will be quickly exterminated.

Insecticides containing malathion, pyrethrum, dimethoate, formothion or fenitrothion may be used at regular intervals as recommended by the manufacturers. Vary the insecticide now and again to avoid letting the aphids build up a resistance to any particular one.

Capsid bugs

These are found mainly on fuchsias growing out of doors and their appearance and life cycle are very similar to those of the aphid. They are very small and mainly greenish in colour. Eggs laid on the plant hatch out into young capsids which feed on the young shoots of the plant, injecting into the shoots a poison which causes discoloration and distortion. Shoots so attacked will invariably be blind.

Spray with fenitrothion, bioresmethrin or gamma-HCH.

Caterpillars

Caterpillars are not often found on fuchsias, but where they are the damage is confined to holes in the leaves.

Spraying with bioresmethrin will eliminate most caterpillars.

Cuckoo spit (froghopper)

The cuckoo spit insect is the young of the froghopper and its presence is indicated by the white froth in which it lives. It feeds on young leaves and shoots. The cuckoo spit insect is very small and yellowish in colour.

Use a pressure sprayer to wash away the froth, then spray with gamma-HCH.

Red spider mite

The red spider mite is so minute that it can scarcely be seen with the naked eye and its presence is often not evident until the first signs of damage appear. The usual symptoms of an attack by red spider mite are mottling of the upper surface of the leaves, and webs on the lower surface, housing the masses of feeding mites. Red spider mite thrives in a hot dry atmosphere but can also be found when conditions are dampish.

Control by spraying with dimethoate, formothion, malathion or rotenone. Smoke fumigants containing gamma-HCH are also effective.

Thrips

These are very small black insects which attack both outdoor and indoor fuchsias. The symptoms of an attack are silvery specks and some distortion of leaves and flowers.

Control by spraying with gamma-HCH or using smoke fumigation.

Vine weevil

It is the larvae of the vine weevil which cause the damage to fuchsias and, as they feed on the roots of the plant, the damage has quite often been done before one is aware that they are present. The adult vine weevil is small, black and beetle-like, and lays its eggs just below the surface of the soil. These hatch out into fat whitish larvae with brown heads, which devour their way through the plant's root system, causing the eventual collapse of the top growth. Although there can be exceptions, the vine weevil is most often found in plants grown in soil-less composts.

Control is by spraying plants with gamma-HCH or using fenitrothion to drench the soil.

Whitefly

The presence of whitefly on greenhouse fuchsias may be obvious in several ways – clouds of them take to the air if one brushes against an infected plant; black sooty mould growing on their honeydew excretions is evidence of eggs; scales may be seen on the undersides of the leaves. The whitefly sucks the sap from the plant which may be badly damaged.

Spraying with dimethoate, gamma-HCH, permethrin or bioresmethrin will kill adult whitefly, and a twice-weekly application should get rid of the young as they hatch out. As with aphids, whitefly can develop a resistance to a particular pesticide and the pesticides used should be varied to prevent this happening.

Fuchsia gall mite

This pest, first identified in the United States in 1981, has not yet reached Britain, but with the increasing numbers of new cultivars being imported, it would seem to be only a matter of time before it does. The signs of the presence of fuchsia gall mite are distortion of the growing tips of the plant, with blistering of the leaves, caused by the injection of poison into the plant by the mite.

Control is achieved by spraying plants with a systemic insecticide based on disulfoton.

Diseases

There are only two diseases currently known to affect fuchsias – botrytis and fuchsia rust.

Botrytis

Grey mould, or *Botrytis cinerea*, is a hairy grey growth which can be found anywhere on the plant – leaves, shoots or flowers – and will, if not checked, take over and kill the plant completely.

Botrytis thrives in damp, cold, poorly ventilated conditions and is more evident in the early part of the year and in the autumn than during the summer months. It usually begins on dead leaves which may have fallen off the plant. It spreads quickly, so one of the main methods of control is to remove all such leaves from the greenhouse as soon as they are seen, and to allow greater ventilation so that there is a good circulation of air around the plants. Spraying with a systemic fungicide, such as Benomyl (Benlate) or Thiram, in addition to the above precautions, should provide good control.

Fuchsia rust

Fuchsia rust (*Pucciniastrum epilobii*) is seen as darkish spots on the upper leaf surface, with orange pustules on the underside. It spreads very quickly from leaf to leaf and plant to plant and, if not dealt with immediately, can soon make its way right through a greenhouse.

Control is achieved by spraying with a good fungicide, such as Thiram or Zineb, at regular weekly intervals. Any plants seen to have the disease should be removed from the greenhouse and either isolated for treatment or burnt. The spores of the disease are rapidly dispersed, either by wind or through the soil, so great care must be taken when infected plants are seen.

One of the host plants of fuchsia rust is the rose bay willowherb (*Epilobium* spp.) and any of these found growing in the vicinity should be destroyed.

Fuchsias may also be subject to a number of physiological disorders which are unconnected with pest or disease attack, but have more to do with general growing problems.

Leaf drop

This is often caused by watering and can be the result of either extreme – too much, or insufficient, water.

Yellowing or discoloured leaves

This could be due to either mineral deficiencies or excesses in the compost.

Leaves yellowish with green veins iron or magnesium deficiency. Spray with sequestrol or Epsom salts (magnesium sulphate).

Leaves small and yellowish green nitrogen deficiency, often caused by the excess use of high potash fertilizers. Use a high nitrogen fertilizer to correct the balance.

Leaf margins brown potash deficiency. Feed with liquid high potash fertilizer.

Leaves scorched or brown an excess of potash, often as a result of over-use of high potash fertilizers. Try to flush out the excess by watering, before changing to a more balanced fertilizer.

Bud drop

Usually due to the plant having been allowed to dry out, or being brought into an atmosphere too dry for it.

Using pesticides and fungicides

Chemicals are dangerous, and, if they are not used correctly in the manner and quantities stated by the manufacturer, they can cause the user problems, as well as the plants being treated.

Always use rubber gloves when mixing up the chemicals and when using a sprayer.

Read the bottle or packet to ascertain the exact quantity to be used in a specific amount of water. Never exceed this in the expectation that a greater quantity will have more effect. As these have already been carefully worked out by the manufacturer, the only effect an increased dose is likely to have is killing the plants as well as the pest or disease.

If you must spray when there is a slight wind blowing, stand with your back to the wind to avoid getting the spray in your face.

Use only sprays recommended for fuchsias. Some fungicides,

while recommended for stronger growing plants, such as roses, have proved damaging to the more tender fuchsia.

Keep the chemicals in the bottles or packets supplied by the manufacturer, and store them in a dry place well out of the reach of children and pets.

Chapter 17

Month-by-month Guide

January

Greenhouse

Old plants from the previous year should now be started into growth. Heat should be increased to about 7°C (45°F) and the plants sprayed over with tepid water to encourage breaking. At this stage plants should not be overwatered, just kept moist, or the new roots could be damaged. Plants which are being grown on the biennial system and have been kept in 11 cm (4½ in), or 12.5 cm (5 in) maximum, pots over the winter will probably still have a good covering of green leaves, but any leaves which turn yellow should be removed. As soon as the plants are growing strongly, they should be potted back into 9 cm (3½ in) or 10 cm (4 in) pots, taking care not to damage the young fibrous roots.

Check that you have sufficient clean pots and fresh compost available for when you start to pot back the old plants, and also ensure there is a good supply of clean labels.

Hygiene remains very important, so dead leaves and other debris must be removed on a regular basis. Remember to ventilate the greenhouse as and when the weather allows, as poor air circulation can encourage botrytis.

Cold frames

Plants buried in a cold frame for the winter should be left for at least another two months unless you have a heated greenhouse to move them to.

Garden plants

As with the cold frame, it is still too early to touch plants in the garden. Branches cut back by frost should be left in place.

February

Greenhouse

The old plants should be breaking well and ready for potting back. Knock the plant out of its pot and remove, as carefully as possible, as much of the old compost as you can without damaging the roots. Replace the plant in a fresh pot at least 2.5 cm (1 in) smaller than the original, using new compost and firming it in lightly. Water sparingly to start with. After a few days, when the plants have settled in, they can be pruned back, but no further than to two buds on each branch unless each of the first buds is breaking, in which case they can be taken right back to one bud. Any suitable material pruned off can be used as cuttings and put into a propagator using a proprietary cuttings compost, or a 50/50 mixture of peat and sharp sand.

March

Greenhouse

Watering of the repotted fuchsias must now be undertaken on a regular basis as and when required, as should spraying with insecticides and fungicides as a preventive measure. As the plants begin to fill their pots with roots, they should be progressively potted on, one pot size at a time. Fuchsia cuttings can be taken throughout the month whenever suitable material is available. Always make sure that plant labels are put in to avoid identification problems later.

As day length increases, pots should be given a quarter turn every couple of days so that they do not become drawn towards the light and grow one-sided.

The shaping of plants, by removing the growing tips, must be regularly attended to. Make sure that the whole plant is done at one time to keep the growth even. Feeding, with a high nitrogen fertilizer, should be done at weekly intervals.

Cuttings are potted up as soon as they have a strong root system, first into small pots – 5 cm (2 in) diameter is sufficient to start with – and then potted on 1 in at a time as necessary. The feeding of cuttings should not begin until they are into 6 cm ($2\frac{1}{2}$ in) or 7.5 cm (3 in) pots, as they grow quickly enough in their early stages and there is normally sufficient feed in proprietary composts for several days' use.

Standards which were overwintered in the greenhouse should be well into growth now and the heads can be pruned and shaped in the same way as for bush plants. Where cuttings are being grown for standards, make sure that the growing tip is not removed and always tie the cutting lightly to a split cane to keep the stem straight.

For hanging baskets and hanging pots, suitable cultivar cuttings, which are into 9 cm ($3\frac{1}{2}$ in) pots, may be planted up into baskets now. Cuttings of plants intended for 9 cm ($3\frac{1}{2}$ in) pot classes at the summer shows should be struck now.

Cold Frames

As the weather and temperature improve, plants in a cold frame can be started into growth. If they were buried, dig them out carefully as growth made at this time is very brittle. As there is still a very good chance of frost in March, the frame should be covered with hessian at night and even during cold days, but wherever possible some ventilation should be given.

Garden
In more sheltered areas there may be some signs of growth on outdoor fuchsias, but it is still too early to prune off the old wood.

April

Greenhouse
Continue pinching out the growing tips and shaping the plants, potting them on as necessary. This applies also to biennial plants, which should be into 15 cm (6 in) or 16 cm (6½ in) pots by this time. Be careful that plants do not dry out as the heat of the sun increases, and continue to turn them regularly. Carry on feeding with a high nitrogen fertilizer until the end of the month.

Hanging basket plants are pinched out in the same way as for bushes, and baskets should be kept in the greenhouse in the meantime.

Young standard whips should be potted on as required, still being tied in to a cane as they grow. The main leaves are left on, but any sideshoots should be removed from the stem as soon as they are large enough to handle.

It may be necessary, in some areas, to consider shading the greenhouse at this time, either by using plastic shading materials or paint-on shading, to avoid plants being scorched by a strong spring sun.

Continue to ventilate the greenhouse. Use pesticides and fungicides regularly, and inspect plants as often as possible to make sure that neither pests nor diseases are present. Cuttings taken this month will root quickly, but always make sure that they are out of direct sunlight.

Cold Frames
Plants in cold frames will be into growth by April and will require the same protection from the sun as greenhouse plants. Watering is important, so do not let them dry out. Cover the frames at night in case of frosts.

Garden
Hardy fuchsias in the garden should all be showing signs of growth, as should hedging plants. Rake in a small amount of general fertilizer around each plant and spray them against pests and diseases. Wait until the end of the month before pruning back the old wood to the ground. With hedging fuchsias, growth will often start from the old wood, but, except in milder areas, the best growth comes from below ground and there is generally little advantage to be gained from leaving about 1 m (4 ft) of top growth.

May

Greenhouse

Continue stopping and potting on as necessary. Baskets may be hung in the greenhouse to take the best advantage of the light, but take care that they do not dry out.

With standard whips, the decision has now to be made as to the eventual height desired, so that the requisite number of sideshoots can be left on before removing the growing tip to form the head.

Feeding should change gradually over the first fortnight, from a high-nitrogen fertilizer to a high-potash one. The easiest method is to feed a 50% dose of each for the first week, then 75% potash to 25% nitrogen during the second, and thereafter to stay with the high potash feed. This helps ripen the plant ready for flowering.

If you intend to exhibit at one of the many fuchsia shows, you will need to look at the dates and then work back 12–14 weeks for double-flowered cultivars, and 10 weeks for single-flowered, to find your final stopping date. For example, for a show on, say, 20 August, the last stopping date for singles will be 4 June, and for doubles as early as 7 May. Don't think that one extra stop will give you a bigger plant with more flowers – it could easily not be in bloom in time!

Cold frame

Conditions here in May are very similar to those in the greenhouse, so plant care is the same. Frame lights can be left open permanently except when there is a frost warning.

Garden

Garden hardies should be well into growth and need only minimal care and attention. Watch out for pests, especially thrips, capsid and caterpillars, and spray accordingly.

June

Greenhouse

Plants are growing very quickly now – keep turning them regularly so that they do not become drawn. Spray weekly to keep pests and diseases at bay – vary your insecticide now and again so that pests do not build up a resistance to any particular one. Watch carefully to see that the plants do not dry out.

Standard heads should be forming in the same way as the bush plants. Keep them staked, but make sure the ties are sufficiently loose not to bite into the stem.

Baskets may be hung outside in a sheltered spot if the weather is good, but not in direct sunlight. Stopping dates for baskets and hanging pots are the same as for bush plants. If the weather is very hot, the greenhouse floor and benches should be damped down.

Leave the door and windows open to keep the temperature down, and make sure that your shading is effective.

Cuttings should be taken this month for growing on the biennial system for next year, provided you will have a minimum temperature of 7°C (40°F) during the winter.

Garden

Although garden hardies need very little trimming to keep them in shape, it is worth while looking them over now and again, stopping where necessary to form a good shape. In hot weather outdoor plants may need a good soaking from time to time to keep them turgid.

New plantings of garden hardies can be made this month. The ground should be prepared as on page 59.

By the end of the month summer bedding fuchsias can be planted out in all but the coldest areas.

July

Greenhouse

Temperatures during July tend to be rather high for fuchsias in the greenhouse unless there is sufficient shading and the floor is regularly damped down, so if you have a shade house or a shaded area in the garden, they would be better out of doors. Make sure, though, that they are not in an area where sudden winds could cause damage.

Insecticide and fungicide spraying may still be necessary, but do not spray plants when the buds have formed as spray will discolour and damage the blooms.

Ensure that plants do not dry out as a check to growth at this time could be difficult to repair.

Biennial cuttings should be potted up as soon as they have rooted, and are best kept out of doors in a cold frame or shaded area.

Cold frame and garden

Plants here need no other treatment than periodic spraying for pests and diseases and, of course, feeding as for greenhouse plants.

August

Greenhouse, frame and garden

Plants are now coming up to their best. Flowering usually begins from the end of July and care must be taken to remove any dead blooms, seedpods and yellowing leaves as they appear.

Pots are full of root and tend to dry out very quickly, so strict attention must be paid to watering. Do not water or spray in the middle of the day when the sun is high, or in the evening when water will lie on the foliage. Morning is by far the best time. Newly planted garden fuchsias, whether for summer bedding or permanent, will also tend to dry out quickly in hot weather, so here again watering must be done when necessary. A mulch of peat after watering will help to keep the soil moist.

September

Fuchsia shows are still being held, particularly in the north of England and Scotland, so the same care and attention has to be paid to the plants if you are exhibiting. Greenhouse plants can be placed out of doors to harden them off and ripen the wood, and this will give an opportunity for cleaning up the greenhouse before settling the plants in again for the winter. Remove all dead leaves, blooms and other debris, and thoroughly disinfect the woodwork and glass.

Hygiene in the garden is also important, so dead leaves, etc., should be removed before they cause disease.

October

Summer bedding fuchsias should be lifted out of the garden as soon as the first frost has touched them. Trim them back very slightly as they will have made a lot of growth in the garden, then spray with a good insecticide and fungicide before putting them back inside. Similarly, those fuchsias which have been standing out of doors in their pots should be sprayed, lightly trimmed and rehoused.

Biennial cuttings should not be potted up further than in 11 cm ($4\frac{1}{2}$ in) pots, and should be stopped all the time to form well-shaped plants ready for next year.

When the early frosts begin, make sure that your greenhouse heater is set to 4°C (40°F) so that the biennials keep growing.

November

There is little to do in the greenhouse this month, other than ensuring that dead leaves and flowers are removed as they fall. Watering should be cut down to a minimum.

December

As with November, this is a quiet month, but ventilation will still be required when weather permits, and hygiene is still equally important.

A List of Recommended Species and Cultivars

This list is intended to help the grower in deciding which fuchsias are best for the various purposes described in the foregoing chapters.

F. magellanica* var. *macrostema
Tube red, short and slender.
Sepals red.
Corolla purple.
Foliage darkish green, small and serrated.
Upright.
Hedging plant to 1.5 m (5 ft).

***F. magellanica* var. *macrostema* 'Variegata'**
Tube and sepals red.
Corolla purple.
Foliage variegated green and silvery.
Upright
Hedging plant to 1.5 m (5 ft).

F. magellanica* var. *molinae
Tube and sepals pale pink.
Corolla lilac-pink, small.
Foliage pale to mid-green.
Upright
Hedging plant to 2 m (6 ft).

F. fulgens
Tube long, dull scarlet
Sepals pale red, greenish-yellow at the tips.
Corolla bright red, small.
Foliage sage green, large leaves.
Upright
Species class, pot 25 cm (10 in).

F. fulgens* var. *gesneriana
Tube orange scarlet.
Sepals green.
Corolla orange scarlet.
Foliage sage green, large.
Upright
Species class, pot 25 cm (10 in) and over.

***F. fulgens* 'Rubra Grandiflora'**
Tube orange scarlet.
Sepals green.
Corolla orange scarlet.
Foliage sage green.
Upright
Species class, pot over 25 cm (10 in).

'Abbé Farges'
Semi-double
Tube light cerise.
Sepals light cerise.
Corolla rosy lilac.
Foliage medium green, small and shiny.
Upright
Bush to 16 cm (6 in) pot or quarter standard.

'Abundance'
Single
Tube and sepals cerise.
Corolla deep purple.
Foliage medium to darkish green.
Upright
Garden hardy to 1 m (4 ft).

'Achievement'
Single
Tube and sepals carmine cerise.
Corolla reddish-purple.
Foliage yellowish-green.
Upright
Bush to 16 cm (6 in) pot or garden hardy to 90 cm (3 ft).

'Aintree'
Single
Tube ivory white.
Sepals ivory, tinted pink, green tips.
Corolla rose madder, touches of white at the base.

Foliage medium green.
Upright
Bush to 16 cm (6 in) pot or standard.

'Alan Ayckbourn'
Single
Tube and sepals baby pink.
Corolla white, bell-shaped.
Foliage medium green.
Upright
Bush to 12.5 cm (5 in) pot or quarter standard.

'Albion'
Single
Tube and sepals neyron rose.
Corolla hyacinth blue.
Foliage medium green.
Upright
Bush to 12.5 cm (5 in) pot.

'Alf Thornley'
Double
Tube rose pink.
Sepals neyron rose.
Corolla white.
Foliage medium green.
Upright
Bush to 16 cm (6 in) pot and summer bedder.

'Alice Hoffman'
Single
Tube and sepals rose.
Corolla white, veined rose.
Foliage dark bronzy green.
Upright
Bush to 12.5 cm (5 in) pot and garden hardy. Suitable for rockery use.

'Alison Ewart'
Single
Tube and sepals neyron rose.
Corolla mauve, flushed pink.
Foliage darkish bronzy green.
Upright
Bush to 16 cm (6½ in) pot, quarter standard, summer bedder.

'Alison Reynolds'
Double
Tube and sepals rose bengal.
Corolla violet to cyclamen purple.
Foliage small, medium green.
Upright.
Bush to 16 cm (6½ in) pot, quarter standard, summer bedder.

'Alwin'
Semi-double
Tube and sepals neyron rose.
Corolla white with red veins.
Foliage small, bright green.
Upright
Bush to 12.5 cm (5 in) pot, hanging pot.

'Amanda Jones'
Single
Tube and sepals white tinged pink.
Corolla pinkish-mauve.
Foliage light green.
Upright
Pot to 11 cm (4½ in), quarter standard.

'Amy Lye'
Single
Tube and sepals creamy white.
Corolla orange cerise.
Foliage dull bronzy green to medium green.
Upright
Quarter to full standard.

'Andenken an Heinrich Henkel'
Triphylla
Tube and sepals rose pink.
Corolla deep rose pink.
Foliage dark olive green with magenta veining.
Upright
Triphylla classes to 16 cm (6½ in) and summer bedder.

'Angela Leslie'
Double
Tube and sepals pink.
Corolla pink with deep pink veins.
Foliage medium green.
Upright
Bush to 16 cm (6½ in) pot.

'Ann H. Tripp'
Single
Tube and sepals white, flushed pink.
Corolla white.
Foliage light to medium green.
Upright
Bush to 16 cm (6½ in) pot or standard.

'Anna of Longleat'
Semi-double
Tube and sepals shell pink.
Corolla lavender.
Foliage darkish green.
Trailer
Basket, half basket or hanging pot.

'Annabel'
Double
Tube and sepals white, flushed pink.
Corolla white.
Foliage light green.
Upright
Bush to 16 cm (6½ in) pot, standard, pyramid.

'Ariel'
Single breviflora type
Tube, sepals and corolla magenta.
Foliage small, deep green.
Upright
Small pot culture.

'Army Nurse'
Semi-double
Tube and sepals carmine.
Corolla bluish-violet, flushed pink.
Foliage medium green.
Upright
Bush to 16 cm (6 in) pot and garden hardy.

'Athela'
Single
Tube and sepals creamy pink.
Corolla salmon pink.
Foliage medium green.
Upright
Bush to 16 cm (6 in) pot or standard.

'Auntie Jinks'
Single
Tube pinkish-red.
Sepals white.
Corolla purple with white shading.
Trailer
Half basket and hanging pot.

'Autumnale'
Single
Tube and sepals scarlet.
Corolla purple.
Foliage yellow and green, changing to coppery red.
Upright
Bush to 16 cm (6½ in) pot, ornamental classes, summer bedder.

'Baker's Tri'
Triphylla
Tube geranium lake.
Sepals venetian pink.
Corolla spinel red.
Foliage medium green.
Upright
Triphylla classes to 16 cm (6½ in) pot, summer bedder.

'Balkonkönigin'
Single
Tube and sepals pale pink.
Corolla pink.
Foliage small, medium green.
Trailer

'Ballet Girl'
Tube and sepals bright cerise red.
Corolla white, veined cerise.
Foliage medium green.
Upright
Bush to 16 cm (6½ in) pot and summer bedder.

'Bambini'
Single
Tube and sepals crimson.
Corolla purple with crimson veins.
Foliage small, medium green.
Upright
Bush to 9 cm (3½ in) pot and summer bedder.

'Barbara'
Single
Tube and sepals pale pink.
Corolla tangerine pink.
Foliage dull green.
Upright
Bush to 16 cm (6½ in) pot, standard, pyramid, pillar, fan, espalier.

'Beacon'
Single
Tube and sepals scarlet.
Corolla mauvish-pink.
Foliage darkish green.
Upright
Bush to 16 cm (6½ in) pot, standard, garden hardy or summer bedder.

'Beacon Rosa'
Single
Tube and sepals rose red.
Corolla rose pink with red veining.
Foliage dark green.
Upright
Bush to 16 cm ($6\frac{1}{2}$ in) pot, half standard or summer bedder.

'Bealings'
Double
Tube and sepals white.
Corolla bright violet.
Foliage medium green.
Upright
Bush to 16 cm ($6\frac{1}{2}$ in) pot, quarter standard.

'Bicentennial'
Double
Tube white.
Sepals Indian orange.
Corolla Indian orange and magenta.
Foliage medium green.
Lax upright
Bush to 16 cm ($6\frac{1}{2}$ in) pot, half basket.

'Billy Green'
Triphylla type
Tube, sepals and corolla pinkish-salmon.
Foliage olive green.
Upright
Bush to 16 cm ($6\frac{1}{2}$ in) pot, standard, summer bedder.

'Blowick'
Single
Tube and sepals white, flushed pink.
Corolla mallow purple.
Foliage medium green.
Upright
Bush to 12.5 cm (5 in) pot.

'Blue Bush'
Single
Tube and sepals rose red.
Corolla bluebird blue with pink veins.
Foliage medium green.
Upright
Garden hardy, hedging plant to 1 m (4 ft).

'Blue Elf'
Single
Tube and sepals rose pink.
Corolla light blue, edged violet.
Foliage olive green with reddish veins.
Upright
Bush to 16 cm ($6\frac{1}{2}$ in) pot and summer bedder.

'Blue Gown'
Double
Tube and sepals scarlet.
Corolla blue with carmine and pink splashes.
Foliage medium green.
Upright
Bush to 16 cm ($6\frac{1}{2}$ in) pot.

'Blue Veil'
Double
Tube and sepals pure white
Corolla lobelia blue.
Foliage medium green.
Lax trailer
Basket or hanging pot.

'Blue Waves'
Double
Tube and sepals pink.
Corolla bluish-violet, splashed and veined carmine.
Foliage light green.
Upright
Bush to 16 cm ($6\frac{1}{2}$ in) pot.

'Blush of Dawn'
Double
Tube and sepals white.
Corolla silvery blue grey.
Foliage medium green.
Lax upright
Bush to 16 cm ($6\frac{1}{2}$ in) pot, basket or hanging pot.

'Bobby Shaftoe'
Semi-double
Tube and sepals white.
Corolla white veined pink.
Foliage light green.
Lax upright
Bush to 16 cm ($6\frac{1}{2}$ in) pot or hanging pot.

'Bobby Wingrove'
Single
Tube and sepals pinkish-red.
Corolla turkey red.
Foliage medium green.
Upright
Bush to 16 cm ($6\frac{1}{2}$ in) pot, quarter standard, summer bedder.

'Bon Accorde'
Single
Tube and sepals white.
Corolla pale purple, flushed white. Held erect.
Foliage medium green.
Upright
Bush to 16 cm ($6\frac{1}{2}$ in) pot or standard.

'Border Queen'
Single
Tube and sepals pink.
Corolla amethyst violet.
Foliage medium green, stems reddish.
Upright
Bush to 16 cm ($6\frac{1}{2}$ in) pot or standard.

'Bornemann's Beste'
Triphylla
Tube, sepals and corolla orange red.
Upright
Triphylla classes or summer bedder.

'Bountiful'
Double
Tube white.
Sepals pale pink.
Corolla white, veined pink.
Foliage medium green.
Upright
Bush to 16 cm ($6\frac{1}{2}$ in) pot.

'Bow Bells'
Single
Tube and sepals white.
Corolla magenta.
Foliage medium green.
Upright
Bush to 16 cm ($6\frac{1}{2}$ in) pot or summer bedder.

'Brighton Belle'
Triphylla
Tube and sepals rosy red.
Corolla salmon pink.
Foliage medium green.
Upright
Bush to 16 cm ($6\frac{1}{2}$ in) pot, triphylla classes.

'Brilliant'
Single
Tube and sepals scarlet
Corolla violet magenta with red veins.
Foliage medium green.
Upright
Standard, pillar, pyramid, summer bedder or garden hardy.

'Brutus'
Single
Tube and sepals crimson cerise.
Corolla deep purple.
Foliage medium green.
Upright
Bush to 16 cm ($6\frac{1}{2}$ in) pot, standard, pyramid, pillar, summer bedder.

'Burning Bush'
Single
Tube and sepals red.
Corolla reddish-purple.
Foliage variegated reddish, cream and yellow.
Upright
Ornamental classes and summer bedder.

'Caledonia'
Single
Tube and sepals cerise.
Corolla crimson.
Foliage medium green.
Low growing, upright.
Bush to 9 cm ($3\frac{1}{2}$ in) pot, summer bedder or garden hardy.

'Cambridge Louie'
Single
Tube and sepals pinkish-orange.
Corolla rosy pink.
Foliage light green, smallish.
Upright
Bush to 16 cm ($6\frac{1}{2}$ in) pot, standard, summer bedder.

'Camelot'
Single
Tube and sepals white.

Corolla white to pale pink.
Foliage medium green.
Upright
Bush to 16 cm (6½ in) pot.

'Cardinal'
Single
Tube and sepals red.
Corolla red.
Foliage medium green.
Upright
Standard, pillar, pyramid, fan or espalier.

'Cardinal Farges'
Semi-double
Tube and sepals pale cerise.
Corolla white, veined cerise.
Foliage medium green, small.
Upright
Bush to 16 cm (6½ in) pot, good 9 cm (3½ in) pot, quarter standard, garden hardy or summer bedder.

'Carl Wallace'
Double
Tube and sepals rosy red.
Corolla violet purple.
Foliage medium green.
Upright
Bush or shrub to 16 cm (6½ in) pot.

'Carlisle Bells'
Single
Tube pale pink.
Sepals white on top, pink underneath.
Corolla bishop's violet.
Foliage darkish green.
Upright
Bush to 16 cm (6½ in) pot or standard, also summer bedder.

'Carmel Blue'
Tube and sepals white, tinged pink.
Corolla blue, maturing to purplish-blue.
Foliage medium green.
Upright
Bush to 16 cm (6½ in) pot.

'Carmen Maria'
Single
Tube, sepals and corolla pink.
Foliage medium green.
Upright
Bush or shrub to 16 cm (6½ in) pot, standard or summer bedder.

'Carnival'
Double
Tube crimson.
Sepals white with green tips.
Corolla bright red.
Foliage medium green.
Trailer
Half basket or hanging pot.

'Carol Roe'
Single
Tube creamy white.
Sepals light pink.
Corolla rosy pink.
Foliage small, medium to darkish green.
Upright
Bush to 11 cm (4½ in) pot, quarter standard.

'Caroline'
Single
Tube pink.
Sepals pale pink.
Corolla pale lavender shading to pale pink.
Foliage medium green.
Upright
Bush or shrub to 16 cm (6½ in) pot.

'Cascade'
Single
Tube and sepals white, flushed carmine.
Corolla rose bengal.
Foliage light to medium green.
Trailer
Basket, half basket or hanging pot.

'Celia Smedley'
Single
Tube and sepals neyron rose.
Corolla bright currant red.
Foliage dull medium green.
Trailer
Bush to 16 cm (6½ in) pot, standard or summer bedder.

'Chang'
Single
Tube and sepals orange red.
Corolla bright orange.
Foliage small, medium green.

Upright
Standard

'Charming'
Single
Tube and sepals carmine.
Corolla purple, maturing to reddish-purple.
Foliage yellowish-green.
Upright
Bush to 16 cm (6½ in) pot, standard, summer bedder or garden hardy.

'Chartwell'
Single
Tube white.
Sepals rhodamine pink.
Corolla wisteria blue.
Foliage medium green.
Upright
Bush to 16 cm (6½ in) pot or summer bedder.

'Checkerboard'
Single
Tube deep red.
Sepals white, red at the base.
Corolla red, white at the base.
Foliage medium to darkish green.
Upright
Bush to 16 cm (6½ in) pot, standard, pillar, fan or espalier.

'Cheviot Princess'
Single
Tube and sepals white.
Corolla ruby red.
Foliage medium green.
Upright
Bush or shrub to 16 cm (6½ in) pot, standard or summer bedder.

'Chillerton Beauty'
Single
Tube and sepals pale pink.
Corolla purple with pink veining.
Foliage glossy medium to darkish green.
Upright
Garden hardy, or hedging plant to 90 cm (3 ft).

'Christmas Elf'
Single
Tube and sepals bright red.
Corolla white with red veins.
Foliage small, dark green.
Small upright.
Small pot culture or bush to 9 cm (3½ in) pot.

'Citation'
Single
Tube and sepals rose pink.
Corolla white with light pink veins.
Foliage medium green.
Upright
Bush to 16 cm (6½ in) pot.

'City of Leicester'
Single
Tube and sepals rose bengal.
Corolla pale violet purple.
Foliage medium green.
Upright
Bush to 16 cm (6½ in) pot, standard or summer bedder.

'C. J. Howlett'
Single
Tube and sepals light scarlet.
Corolla pale cerise purple.
Foliage medium green.
Upright
Bush to 16 cm (6½ in) pot, summer bedder or garden hardy.

'Cliff's Hardy'
Single
Tube and sepals crimson.
Corolla campanula violet.
Foliage small, darkish green.
Upright
Bush to 16 cm (6½ in) pot or garden hardy.

'Cliff's Unique'
Double
Tube light pink.
Sepals white, flushed pink, green tips.
Corolla gentian blue to violet pink.
Foliage medium green.
Upright
Bush to 16 cm (6½ in) pot or quarter standard.

'Clifton Beauty'
Double
Tube white.

Sepals creamy pink.
Corolla rosy purple with crimson edges and salmon streaks.
Foliage medium green.
Trailer
Basket, half basket or hanging pot.

'Clipper'
Single
Tube and sepals scarlet cerise.
Corolla claret red.
Foliage medium green.
Bush to 16 cm (6½ in) pot or standard.

'Cloth of Gold'
Single
Tube and sepals red.
Corolla purple.
Foliage golden yellow, ageing to green and with a bronze flush. The underside is reddish.
Ornamental bush to 16 cm (6½ in) pot or summer bedder.

'Cloverdale Jewel'
Semi-double
Tube and sepals neyron rose.
Corolla wisteria blue with rose pink veins.
Foliage small, medium green.
Bush, best in 9 cm (3½ in) pot or summer bedder.

'Cloverdale Pearl'
Single
Tube white.
Sepals rhodamine pink.
Corolla white with pink veins.
Foliage darkish green, small.
Bush to 16 cm (6½ in) pot, standard or summer bedder.

'Cloverdale Pride'
Single
Tube pale pink.
Sepals rose bengal.
Corolla cyclamen purple.
Foliage medium green.
Bush to 16 cm (6½ in) pot or quarter standard.

'Cloverdale Star'
Single
Tube and sepals white.
Corolla wisteria blue.
Foliage medium green.
Bush or shrub to 16 cm (6½ in) pot.

'Coachman'
Single
Tube and sepals salmon pink.
Corolla orange vermilion.
Foliage light green.
Bush or shrub to 16 cm (6½ in) pot or half basket.

'Collingwood'
Double
Tube and sepals pale pink.
Corolla pure white.
Foliage medium green.
Bush to 16 cm (6½ in) pot or summer bedder.

'Come Dancing'
Double
Tube and sepals deep pink.
Corolla magenta rose.
Foliage bright green.
Bush to 16 cm (6½ in) pot or half basket.

'Constance'
Double
Tube and sepals pale pink.
Corolla rosy-mauve.
Foliage medium green.
Upright
Bush to 16 cm (6½ in) pot, standard, fan, espalier, pillar or summer bedder.

'Coquet Bell'
Single
Tube and sepals rose madder.
Corolla pale mauve with red veins, bell-shaped.
Foliage medium green.
Upright
Bush to 16 cm (6½ in) pot or standard.

'Coquet Dale'
Double
Tube pinkish-white.
Sepals neyron rose.
Corolla lilac.
Foliage medium green.
Upright

Bush to 16 cm ($6\frac{1}{2}$ in) pot, standard or summer bedder.

'Corallina'
Single
Tube and sepals carmine.
Corolla purple.
Foliage darkish bronzy green.
Arching upright.
Garden hardy.

'Countess of Aberdeen'
Single
Tube creamy white.
Sepals white.
Corolla white.
Foliage small, medium green.
Upright
Bush or shrub in pots up to 16 cm ($6\frac{1}{2}$ in), best in 9 cm ($3\frac{1}{2}$ in), also as quarter standard.

'Countess of Maritza'
Double
Tube and sepals pale pink.
Corolla lilac.
Foliage medium green.
Upright
Bush up to 16 cm ($6\frac{1}{2}$ in) pot or standard.

'Crackerjack'
Single
Tube and sepals white flushed pink.
Corolla pale mauve blue with pink veins.
Foliage light green with crimson veining.
Trailer
Basket, half basket or hanging pot.

'Cropwell Butler'
Single
Tube and sepals rosy red.
Corolla campanula violet.
Foliage medium to darkish green.
Upright
Bush or shrub up to 16 cm ($6\frac{1}{2}$ in) pot, quarter standard or summer bedder.

'Curtain Call'
Double
Tube pale carmine to white.
Sepals white flushed pink.
Corolla rosy cerise.
Foliage medium green.
Trailer
Basket, half basket or hanging pot.

'Daisy Bell'
Single
Tube long, white.
Sepals pale orange with apple green tips.
Corolla vermilion shading to orange.
Foliage small, medium green.
Trailer
Basket, half basket or hanging pot.

'Dalton'
Single
Tube and sepals flesh pink.
Corolla soft pink.
Foliage medium green.
Upright
Bush up to 11 cm ($4\frac{1}{2}$ in) pot or summer bedder.

'Dark Eyes'
Double
Tube and sepals deep red.
Corolla deep violet blue.
Foliage medium to darkish green.
Upright
Bush to 16 cm ($6\frac{1}{2}$ in) pot.

'Derby Imp'
Single
Tube and sepals crimson red.
Corolla violet blue.
Foliage small, medium green.
Stiff trailer or upright.
Bush to 16 cm ($6\frac{1}{2}$ in) pot, basket or quarter standard.

'Display'
Single
Tube pink
Sepals deep rose pink.
Corolla deep cerise pink.
Foliage dullish medium green.
Upright
Bush to 16 cm ($6\frac{1}{2}$ in) pot, standard, pillar, pyramid or summer bedder.

'Doctor Brendan Freeman'
Single

Tube pale pink.
Sepals rhodamine pink.
Corolla white.
Foliage medium green.
Upright
Bush or shrub to 16 cm (6½ in) pot, standard or summer bedder.

'Dollar Princess'
Double
Tube and sepals cerise.
Corolla purple, cerise at the base.
Foliage medium to darkish green.
Upright
Bush or shrub to 16 cm (6½ in) pot, quarter standard, summer bedder or garden hardy.

'Donna May'
Single
Tube and sepals neyron rose.
Corolla opens violet purple, ageing to cyclamen purple.
Foliage darkish green.
Upright
Bush or shrub to 16 cm (6½ in) pot or quarter standard.

'Doreen Redfern'
Single
Tube and sepals white
Corolla methyl violet.
Foliage darkish green.
Upright
Bush to 16 cm (6½ in) pot, standard or summer bedder.

'Dorothea Flower'
Single
Tube and sepals white flushed pink.
Corolla deep lavender blue.
Foliage medium green.
Upright
Bush to 16 cm (6½ in) pot, standard or summer bedder.

'Dr Foster'
Single
Tube and sepals scarlet.
Corolla violet purple.
Foliage medium green.
Upright
Garden hardy or summer bedder.

'Dr Topinard'
Single
Tube and sepals rose red.
Corolla pure white with rose veining.
Foliage dark green.
Upright
Bush to 16 cm (6½ in) pot or quarter standard.

'Drame'
Semi-double
Tube and sepals scarlet.
Corolla purplish-red.
Foliage medium green, small.
Upright
Garden hardy.

'Dulcie Elizabeth'
Double
Tube and sepals rose pink.
Corolla lavender blue with pink flecks.
Foliage medium green.
Upright
Bush to 16 cm (6½ in) pot or summer bedder.

'Dunrobin Bedder'
Single
Tube bright red.
Sepals scarlet.
Corolla violet purple.
Foliage small, medium green.
Upright
Small bush to 11 cm (4½ in) pot or garden hardy.

'Dusky Beauty'
Single
Tube and sepals neyron rose.
Corolla pale purple with pinkish cast and edges.
Foliage small, darkish green.
Upright
Bush or shrub to 16 cm (6½ in) pot, quarter standard or summer bedder.

'Eden Lady'
Single
Tube pale rose pink.
Sepals amaranth rose.
Corolla hyacinth blue.
Foliage medium green.
Upright
Bush to 16 cm (6½ in) pot or quarter standard.

'Edith Emery'
Semi-double
Tube and sepals white.
Corolla amethyst violet.
Foliage spinach green.
Upright
Bush to 16 cm ($6\frac{1}{2}$ in) pot, standard, fan or summer bedder.

'Edna May'
Single
Tube and sepals white, flushed pink.
Corolla cream.
Foliage darkish green.
Upright
Bush to 12.5 cm (5 in) pot or quarter standard.

'Eleanor Clark'
Single
Tube and sepals pale phlox pink.
Corolla shell pink.
Foliage light to medium green.
Upright
Bush to 16 cm ($6\frac{1}{2}$ in) pot or quarter standard.

'Eleanor Leytham'
Single
Tube and sepals pinkish-white.
Corolla pink, edged deeper pink.
Foliage small, glossy medium green.
Upright
Bush to 9 cm ($3\frac{1}{2}$ in) pot or quarter standard.

'Elfriede Ott'
Triphylla type
Tube, sepals and corolla salmon pink.
Foliage dark green.
Upright
Triphylla classes.

'Emile de Wildeman' (syn. 'Fascination')
Double
Tube and sepals carmine red.
Corolla pink, veined cerise.
Foliage medium green.
Upright
Bush to 16 cm ($6\frac{1}{2}$ in) pot, standard or summer bedder.

'Empress of Prussia'
Single
Tube and sepals scarlet.
Corolla magenta to scarlet lake.
Foliage medium to darkish green.
Upright
Garden hardy.

'Enfante Prodigue' (syn. 'Prodigy')
Double
Tube and sepals crimson.
Corolla bluish-purple.
Foliage small, medium to darkish green.
Upright
Garden hardy.

'Estelle Marie'
Single
Tube greenish-white.
Sepals white with green tips.
Corolla pale violet purple.
Foliage darkish green.
Upright
Bush or shrub to 16 cm ($6\frac{1}{2}$ in) pot, standard or summer bedder. Also good in 9 cm ($3\frac{1}{2}$ in) pots.

'Eva Boerg'
Semi-double
Tube greenish-white.
Sepals white, flushed pink.
Corolla pinkish-purple, splashed pink.
Foliage pale to medium green.
Lax upright.
Bush to 16 cm ($6\frac{1}{2}$ in) pots, standard, basket, half basket, hanging pot or summer bedder.

'Evensong'
Single
Tube pink.
Sepals white, tipped green.
Corolla white, bell-shaped.
Foliage pale green.
Upright
Bush to 16 cm ($6\frac{1}{2}$ in) pot or summer bedder.

'Excalibur'
Single
Tube and sepals pale pink.
Corolla baby pink.
Foliage medium to darkish green.
Upright
Bush to 9 cm ($3\frac{1}{2}$ in) pot or quarter standard.

'Fiona'
Single
Tube and sepals white.
Corolla blue, maturing to reddish-purple.
Foliage medium green.
Upright
Bush to 16 cm ($6\frac{1}{2}$ in) pot or standard.

'First Kiss'
Semi-double
Tube and sepals creamy white.
Corolla pale rose pink.
Foliage medium green.
Lax upright.
Bush to 16 cm ($6\frac{1}{2}$ in) pot or hanging pot.

'Flash'
Single
Tube and sepals light magenta red.
Corolla small, red.
Foliage light green, small.
Upright
Garden hardy or summer bedder.

'Flirtation Waltz'
Double
Tube and sepals white.
Corolla pale pink.
Foliage pale to medium green.
Upright
Bush or shrub to 16 cm ($6\frac{1}{2}$ in) pot or quarter standard.

'Florence Mary Abbott'
Single
Tube white to pale cream.
Sepals white.
Corolla white.
Foliage bright green.
Upright
Bush or shrub to 16 cm ($6\frac{1}{2}$ in) pot or quarter standard.

'Flying Scotsman'
Double
Tube white.
Sepals dark pink.
Corolla red with white streaks.
Foliage medium green.
Upright
Standard or summer bedder.

'Forward Look'
Single
Tube and sepals pink.
Corolla violet blue.
Foliage medium green.
Upright
Bush to 16 cm ($6\frac{1}{2}$ in) pot or summer bedder.

'Frank Unsworth'
Double
Tube and sepals white.
Corolla white, flushed pink.
Foliage medium to darkish green.
Trailer
Basket, half basket or hanging pot.

'Frome in Bloom'
Single
Tube and sepals bright red.
Corolla white with red veins.
Foliage dark green.
Trailer
Basket, half basket or hanging pot.

'Frosted Flame'
Single
Tube and sepals white, flushed pink.
Corolla bright flame red.
Foliage bright green.
Trailer
Basket, half basket or hanging pot.

'Garden News'
Double
Tube and sepals pink.
Corolla magenta rose and rose pink.
Foliage medium green.
Upright
Bush or shrub to 16 cm ($6\frac{1}{2}$ in) pot, summer bedder or garden hardy.

'Gartenmeister Bonstedt'
Triphylla
Tube, sepals and corolla brick red.
Foliage dark bronzy reddish-green.
Upright
Triphylla classes or summer bedder.

'General Monk'
Double
Tube and sepals cerise.
Corolla bluish-purple.
Foliage medium green, small.

Upright
Bush to 16 cm (6½ in) pot or summer bedder.

'Genii'
Single
Tube and sepals cerise.
Corolla dark purple, ageing to reddish-purple.
Foliage pale to medium yellowish-green when grown out of doors, but green when shaded.
Upright
Bush or shrub to 16 cm (6½ in) pot, summer bedder or garden hardy.

'Glenby'
Double
Tube and sepals rose madder.
Corolla amethyst violet.
Foliage medium green.
Upright
Bush to 16 cm (6½ in) pot, particularly good in a 9 cm (3½ in) pot, summer bedder or quarter standard.

'Glororum'
Single
Tube and sepals neyron rose.
Corolla amethyst violet, bell-shaped.
Foliage medium green with reddish stems.
Upright
Bush to 16 cm (6½ in) pot or standard.

'Golden Anniversary'
Double
Tube greenish-white.
Sepals white.
Corolla deep blackish-purple, fading to royal purple.
Foliage new growth is light green to greenish-gold, fading to light green.
Trailer
Basket or hanging pot.

'Golden Arrow'
Triphylla type
Tube and sepals orange.
Corolla tangerine orange.
Foliage medium to darkish green.
Lax trailer.
Hanging pot.

'Golden Border Queen'
Foliage bright yellow.
Growth as for 'Border Queen'

'Golden Eden Lady'
Foliage bright yellow.
Growth as for 'Eden Lady'

'Golden Marinka'
Single
Tube and sepals deep red.
Corolla slightly deeper red.
Foliage variegated green and yellow with red veins.
Trailer
Basket, half basket or hanging pot.

'Golden Treasure'
Single
Tube and sepals scarlet.
Corolla magenta purple.
Foliage variegated green and yellow.
Upright
Ornamental classes or summer bedder.

'Graf Witte'
Single
Tube and sepals carmine.
Corolla purple with cerise veins.
Foliage yellowish-green.
Upright
Garden hardy or bush up to 16 cm (6½ in) pot.

'Grayrigg'
Single
Tube white.
Sepals white with pink flush.
Corolla soft pink.
Foliage small, pale green.
Upright
Garden hardy or hedging plant to 90 cm (3 ft).

'Gruss aus dem Bodethal'
Single
Tube and sepals crimson.
Corolla very dark purple.
Foliage small, medium green.
Upright
Bush to 16 cm (6½ in) pot or summer bedder.

'Heidi Ann'
Double
Tube crimson.
Sepals crimson cerise.
Corolla bright lilac purple.
Foliage small, medium green.
Upright
Bush to 16 cm ($6\frac{1}{2}$ in) pot, quarter standard or summer bedder.

'Heidi Weiss'
Double
Tube and sepals crimson.
Corolla white with scarlet veins.
Foliage small, darkish green.
Upright
Bush to 16 cm ($6\frac{1}{2}$ in) pot, quarter standard or summer bedder.

'Herald'
Single
Tube and sepals scarlet.
Corolla deep bluish-purple with cerise veining.
Foliage medium green, veins crimson.
Upright
Bush to 16 cm ($6\frac{1}{2}$ in) pot, standard, summer bedder or garden hardy.

'Hidcote Beauty'
Single
Tube and sepals creamy white.
Corolla pale salmon pink.
Foliage small, dull pale green.
Upright
Bush to 16 cm ($6\frac{1}{2}$ in) pot, quarter standard or summer bedder.

'Howlett's Hardy'
Single
Tube and sepals scarlet.
Corolla bright violet purple.
Foliage medium green.
Upright
Garden hardy or summer bedder.

'Ian Leedham'
Semi-double
Tube neyron rose.
Sepals crimson.
Corolla tyrian purple.
Foliage medium green.
Trailer
Basket, half basket or hanging pot.

'Iceberg'
Single
Tube carmine with red stripes.
Sepals white.
Corolla white.
Foliage medium to dark green.
Upright
Bush to 16 cm ($6\frac{1}{2}$ in) pot, standard or summer bedder.

'Icecap'
Single to semi-double.
Tube and sepals bright red.
Corolla white with cerise veins.
Foliage medium to darkish green.
Upright
Bush to 16 cm ($6\frac{1}{2}$ in) pot, standard or summer bedder.

'Iced Champagne'
Single
Tube and sepals pale pink.
Corolla pale pink with darker veins.
Foliage medium green with red veins.
Lax upright.
Bush to 16 cm ($6\frac{1}{2}$ in) pot, very good in 9 cm ($3\frac{1}{2}$ in) pot.

'Impudence'
Single
Tube and sepals carmine red.
Corolla white with carmine veins, petals spread out.
Foliage medium green.
Upright
Bush to 16 cm ($6\frac{1}{2}$ in) pot.

'Indian Maid'
Double
Tube and sepals scarlet.
Corolla royal purple.
Foliage darkish green.
Upright
Bush to 16 cm ($6\frac{1}{2}$ in) pot or half basket.

'Isle of Mull'
Single
Tube light magenta.
Sepals baby pink.
Corolla rose magenta splashed pink.
Foliage medium green.
Upright
Bush to 16 cm ($6\frac{1}{2}$ in) pot or standard.

'Jack Acland'
Semi-double
Tube and sepals bright pink.
Corolla dark rose red.
Foliage medium green.
Upright
Bush to 16 cm ($6\frac{1}{2}$ in) pot or standard.

'Jack Shahan'
Single
Tube and sepals rose bengal.
Corolla rose pink.
Foliage medium green.
Trailer
Basket, half basket or hanging pot.

'Jean Ewart'
Single
Tube and sepals china rose.
Corolla amaranth rose.
Foliage medium green.
Upright
Bush to 16 cm ($6\frac{1}{2}$ in) pot, quarter standard or summer bedder.

'Joan Cooper'
Single
Tube and sepals pale rose pink.
Corolla cherry red.
Foliage light green.
Upright
Garden hardy or summer bedder.

'Joan Pacey'
Single
Tube white, tinged pink.
Sepals pink.
Corolla phlox pink.
Foliage light to medium green.
Upright
Bush to 16 cm ($6\frac{1}{2}$ in) pot, standard or summer bedder.

'John Maynard Scales'
Triphylla
Tube, sepals and corolla orange.
Foliage sage green.
Upright
Triphylla classes to 16 cm ($6\frac{1}{2}$ in) pot.

'Joy Bielby'
Double
Tube white with neyron rose stripes.
Sepals white, flushed neyron rose.
Corolla white.
Foliage medium green.
Trailer
Basket, half basket or hanging pot.

'Joy Patmore'
Single
Tube and sepals white.
Corolla pinkish cerise.
Foliage medium green.
Upright
Bush or shrub to 16 cm ($6\frac{1}{2}$ in) pot, standard or summer bedder.

'Karen Bielby'
Single
Tube venetian pink.
Sepals carmine rose.
Corolla fuchsia purple.
Foliage medium green.
Trailer
Basket or hanging pot.

'Kaye Elizabeth'
Double
Tube and sepals scarlet.
Corolla dark purple.
Foliage small, medium green.
Low growing, upright.
Garden hard (rockery).

'Kegworth Beauty'
Single
Tube and sepals white.
Corolla amaranth rose.
Foliage medium green.
Upright
Bush to 16 cm ($6\frac{1}{2}$ in) pot or standard.

'Kegworth Carnival'
Double
Tube and sepals white.
Corolla tyrian purple.
Foliage medium green.
Trailer
Hanging pot or basket.

'Kegworth Supreme'
Single
Tube and sepals empire rose.
Corolla fuchsia purple.
Foliage dark green.
Upright

Bush to 16 cm (6½ in) pot or standard.

'Ken Jennings'
Single
Tube and Sepals rhodamine pink.
Corolla tyrian purple.
Foliage medium green, smallish.
Upright
Bush to 12.5 cm (5 in) pot or quarter standard, also summer bedder.

'Kerry Ann'
Single
Tube and sepals neyron rose.
Corolla aster violet.
Foliage medium green.
Upright
Bush to 16 cm (6½ in) pot or quarter standard.

'Keystone'
Single
Tube pink.
Sepals pale pink.
Corolla very pale pink.
Foliage medium green.
Upright
Bush to 12.5 cm (5 in) pot or summer bedder.

'Khada'
Single
Tube and sepals rose red.
Corolla white with rose veining.
Foliage medium green.
Upright
Bush to 12.5 cm (5 in) pot, best in 9 cm (3½ in) pot, quarter standard or summer bedder.

'King's Ransom'
Double
Tube and sepals white.
Corolla bright violet purple.
Foliage medium green.
Upright
Bush to 16 cm (6½ in) pot or standard.

'Kolding Perle'
Single
Tube and sepals white.
Corolla bright pink, overlaid with salmon orange.
Foliage pale to medium green.
Upright
Bush to 16 cm (6½ in) pot, standard or summer bedder.

'Koralle'
Triphylla type
Tube, sepals and corolla salmon orange.
Foliage deep sage green.
Upright
Bush to 16 cm (6½ in) pot, triphylla classes or summer bedder.

'La Campanella'
Semi-double
Tube and sepals white, flushed pink.
Corolla imperial purple, ageing to lavender.
Foliage small, medium green.
Lax upright.
Basket, half basket or hanging pot.

'Lady Boothby'
Single
Tube and sepals crimson.
Corolla very dark purple.
Foliage darkish green, small.
Upright
Fan or espalier.

'Lady Isobel Barnett'
Single
Tube and sepals rose red.
Corolla rosy purple with imperial purple edges.
Foliage dull light to medium green.
Upright
Bush to 16 cm (6½ in) pot, standard or summer bedder.

'Lady Kathleen Spence'
Single
Tube white to pale pink.
Sepals whitish-rose.
Corolla lavender.
Foliage medium green.
Lax upright
Bush to 16 cm (6½ in) pot.

'Lady Patricia Mountbatten'
Single
Tube and sepals pale pink to white.
Corolla pale lavender.
Foliage medium green.

Upright
Bush to 16 cm ($6\frac{1}{2}$ in) pot.

'Lady Ramsey'
Single
Tube and sepals flesh pink.
Corolla violet, bell-shaped.
Foliage dull medium green.
Upright
Bush or shrub to 16 cm ($6\frac{1}{2}$ in) pot or quarter standard.

'Lady Thumb'
Semi-double
Tube and sepals carmine.
Corolla white with pink veins.
Foliage small, medium green.
Upright
Bush to 16 cm ($6\frac{1}{2}$ in) pot, quarter standard, summer bedder or garden hardy.

'Lakeland Princess'
Single
Tube carmine.
Sepals white, flushed carmine.
Corolla spectrum violet.
Foliage medium green.
Bush to 16 cm ($6\frac{1}{2}$ in) pot, standard or summer bedder.

'Lakeside'
Single to semi-double.
Tube and sepals bright pink to neyron rose.
Corolla bluish-violet.
Foliage small, medium green.
Basket, half basket or hanging pot.

'Lancelot'
Single
Tube and sepals red.
Corolla white with red veins.
Foliage medium green.
Bush or shrub to 16 cm ($6\frac{1}{2}$ in) pot, quarter standard or summer bedder.

'Lena Dalton'
Double
Tube and sepals pale pink.
Corolla lavender blue, ageing to rosy-mauve.
Foliage darkish green.
Bush to 16 cm ($6\frac{1}{2}$ in) pot, quarter standard or summer bedder.

'Leonora'
Single
Tube and sepals pink.
Corolla pink, bell-shaped.
Foliage medium green.
Bush to 16 cm ($6\frac{1}{2}$ in) pot, standard or summer bedder.

'Leonora Rose'
Single
Tube and sepals pale pink.
Corolla blush pink.
Foliage medium green.
Bush to 16 cm ($6\frac{1}{2}$ in) or standard.

'Liebriez'
Single
Tube pale cerise pink.
Sepals cerise pink.
Corolla pink with deeper pink veining.
Foliage small, medium green.
Bush to 16 cm ($6\frac{1}{2}$ in) pot, good in 9 cm ($3\frac{1}{2}$ in) pot, quarter standard or summer bedder.

'Lilac Lustre'
Double
Tube and sepals rose red.
Corolla powder blue to lilac.
Foliage bright green.
Bush to 16 cm ($6\frac{1}{2}$ in) pot, standard or summer bedder.

'Linda Goulding'
Single
Tube white.
Sepals pink.
Corolla white with pale pink veining, bell-shaped.
Bush to 16 cm ($6\frac{1}{2}$ in) pot or quarter standard.

'Lindisfarne'
Semi-double
Tube pale shell pink.
Sepals pale pink.
Corolla dark violet, deeper at the edges.
Foliage medium green.
Upright
Bush to 16 cm ($6\frac{1}{2}$ in) pot, standard or summer bedder.

'Little Catbells'
Single, Encliandra type.

Tube white.
Sepals rose pink.
Corolla white, changing to rose.
Foliage light green, very small.
Upright
Small pot culture.

'Little Jewel'
Single
Tube and sepals dark carmine.
Corolla light purple, variegated carmine.
Foliage medium green.
Upright
Bush to 16 cm (6½ in) pot or standard.

'Lochinver'
Double
Tube and sepals pale pink.
Corolla imperial purple.
Foliage dark green.
Upright
Bush to 16 cm (6½ in) pot, standard or summer bedder.

'Loeky'
Single
Tube and sepals rose red.
Corolla rosy-lilac, with reddish veining.
Foliage medium green.
Upright
Bush or shrub to 16 cm (6½ in) pot, quarter standard or summer bedder.

'Lord Roberts'
Single
Tube and sepals scarlet cerise.
Corolla dark purple with scarlet veining.
Foliage medium green with red veins.
Upright
Bush to 16 cm (6½ in) pot, standard or summer bedder.

'Lotty Hobby'
Breviflora type
Tube, sepals and corolla dark red.
Foliage medium to dark green, small.
Upright
Small pot culture or garden hardy.

'Loveliness'
Single
Tube and sepals waxy-white.
Corolla rosy cerise.
Foliage light to medium green.
Upright
Bush or shrub to 16 cm (6½ in) pot, standard or summer bedder.

'Lustre'
Single
Tube and sepals creamy white.
Corolla salmon pink.
Foliage small, dull green.
Upright
Bush to 16 cm (6½ in) pot, good in 9 cm (3½ in) pot, standard or summer bedder.

'Lye's Unique'
Single
Tube and sepals waxy white.
Corolla salmon orange.
Foliage dull green.
Upright
Bush to 16 cm (6½ in) pot, standard or summer bedder.

'Madame Cornelissen'
Single to semi-double.
Tube and sepals crimson.
Corolla white with crimson veining.
Foliage dark green, small.
Upright
Bush to 16 cm (6½ in) pot, quarter standard or garden hardy.

'Mantilla'
Triphylla type.
Tube, sepals and corolla deep carmine.
Foliage bronzy green.
Trailer
Basket, half basket or hanging pot.

'Margaret'
Double
Tube and sepals carmine red.
Corolla violet purple.
Foliage shiny medium green.
Upright
Garden hardy or hedging plant to 90 cm (3 ft).

'Margaret Brown'
Single

Tube and sepals rose pink.
Corolla pale rose pink.
Foliage small, light green.
Upright
Garden hardy or summer bedder.

'Margaret Pilkington'
Single
Tube and sepals waxy white.
Corolla bishop's violet, ageing to mallow purple.
Foliage medium green.
Upright
Bush or shrub to 16 cm (6½ in) pot, standard, hanging pot or summer bedder.

'Margaret Roe'
Single
Tube pale rose pink.
Sepals rose red with green tips.
Corolla pale violet purple with pink veins.
Foliage medium green.
Upright
Bush or shrub to 16 cm (6½ in) pot, standard or summer bedder.

'Margaret Rose'
Single
Tube and sepals neyron rose.
Corolla neyron rose with picotee edge of spinel red.
Foliage medium green.
Upright
Bush to 16 cm (6½ in) pot, standard or summer bedder.

'Margery Blake'
Single
Tube and sepals scarlet.
Corolla reddish-purple.
Foliage small, medium green.
Upright
Garden hardy or summer bedder.

'Marin Glow'
Single
Tube white.
Sepals white with green tips.
Corolla imperial purple.
Foliage medium green.
Upright
Bush to 16 cm (6½ in) pot, quarter standard or summer bedder.

'Marinka'
Single
Tube and sepals red.
Corolla dark red.
Foliage medium to darkish green, with red veining.
Trailer
Basket, half basket or hanging pot.

'Mary'
Triphylla
Tube, sepals and corolla brilliant scarlet red.
Foliage dark greyish-green with reddish-purple veins.
Upright
Triphylla classes, bush to 16 cm (6½ in) pot, or summer bedder.

'Maureen Munro'
Single
Tube and sepals neyron rose.
Corolla amethyst violet.
Foliage small, medium green.
Upright
Bush, best in 9 cm (3½ in) pot, quarter standard or summer bedder.

'Mauve Beauty'
Double
Tube and sepals cerise.
Corolla mauve lilac, ageing to pale purple with cerise veins.
Foliage medium green, new growth reddish.
Upright
Bush to 16 cm (6½ in) pot, standard or summer bedder.

'Max Jaffa'
Single
Tube and sepals orient pink.
Corolla mandarin red.
Foliage darkish green.
Lax upright
Small bush to 11 cm (4½ in) pot or hanging pot.

'Mayfield'
Single
Tube red.
Sepals deep rose pink.
Corolla violet blue with darker edges.

Foliage medium green.
Upright
Bush to 16 cm ($6\frac{1}{2}$ in) pot, standard or summer bedder.

'Mazda'
Single
Tube and sepals orange pink.
Corolla carmine orange.
Foliage medium to darkish green.
Upright
Bush to 16 cm ($6\frac{1}{2}$ in) pot, standard or summer bedder.

'Melody'
Single
Tube and sepals pale rose pink.
Corolla pale cyclamen purple.
Foliage bright green.
Upright
Bush to 16 cm ($6\frac{1}{2}$ in) pot, standard or summer bedder.

'Mephisto'
Single
Tube and sepals scarlet.
Corolla crimson red.
Foliage medium green.
Upright
Garden hardy or summer bedder.

'Micky Goult'
Single
Tube pink.
Sepals pink, turning to deeper pink.
Corolla mallow purple.
Foliage medium green
Upright
Bush up to 16 cm ($6\frac{1}{2}$ in) pot, standard or summer bedder.

'Mieke Meursing'
Single to semi-double
Tube and sepals carmine red.
Corolla rose pink with deeper veining.
Foliage medium green.
Upright
Bush or shrub to 16 cm ($6\frac{1}{2}$ in) pot, standard or summer bedder.

'Minirose'
Single
Tube and sepals white with pinkish flush.
Corolla reddish-purple, rose red at the base.
Foliage medium green.
Upright
Bush to 12.5 cm (5 in) pot, quarter standard or summer bedder.

'Mipam'
Single
Tube and sepals pale carmine.
Corolla magenta pink.
Foliage medium green.
Upright
Bush or shrub to 16 cm ($6\frac{1}{2}$ in) pot, standard or summer bedder.

'Miss California'
Semi-double
Tube and sepals pink.
Corolla white with pink veins.
Foliage medium green.
Upright
Bush to 16 cm ($6\frac{1}{2}$ in) pot or standard.

'Mission Bells'
Single
Tube and sepals scarlet.
Corolla purple, bell-shaped.
Foliage medium green.
Upright
Bush to 16 cm ($6\frac{1}{2}$ in) pot or standard.

'Molesworth'
Double
Tube and sepals cerise.
Corolla white, veined cerise.
Foliage medium green.
Trailer
Basket, half basket or hanging pot.

'Monsieur Thibault'
Single
Tube and sepals cerise red.
Corolla magenta with cerise veins.
Foliage darkish green.
Upright
Bush to 16 cm ($6\frac{1}{2}$ in) pot, standard or summer bedder.

'Moonlight Sonata'
Single
Tube and sepals pink.
Corolla pale purple.

Foliage medium green.
Lax upright.
Bush to 16 cm (6½ in) pot, standard or hanging pot.

'Mr A. Huggett'
Single
Tube and sepals scarlet.
Corolla pinkish-purple, deeper at the petal edges.
Foliage medium green.
Upright
Bush to 16 cm (6½ in) pot, quarter standard or summer bedder.

'Mr W. Rundle'
Single
Tube and sepals rose pink.
Corolla orange vermilion.
Foliage small, medium green.
Lax bushy upright.
Standard or summer bedder.

'Mrs Lawrence Lyon'
Single
Tube and sepals ivory white.
Corolla pale fuchsia purple.
Foliage medium green.
Upright
Bush to 12.5 cm (5 in) pot, quarter standard or summer bedder.

'Mrs Lovell Swisher'
Single
Tube pink.
Sepals pinkish-white.
Corolla pale carmine red.
Foliage medium green.
Upright
Bush to 16 cm (6½ in) pot, standard, pillar, fan, espalier, summer bedder.

'Mrs Marshall'
Single
Tube and sepals creamy white.
Corolla rosy cerise.
Foliage dull medium green.
Upright
Bush or shrub to 16 cm (6½ in) pot, standard or summer bedder.

'Mrs Popple'
Single
Tube and sepals scarlet.
Corolla violet purple.
Foliage dark green.
Upright
Bush to 16 cm (6½ in) pot, standard, summer bedder or garden hardy.

'Mrs W. P. Wood'
Single
Tube and sepals pale pink.
Corolla white.
Foliage small, light green.
Garden hardy or hedging plant to 1 m (4 ft).

'Mrs W. Rundle'
Single
Tube pale waxy rose.
Sepals flesh pink with green tips.
Corolla orange crimson.
Foliage light green.
Upright
Summer bedder.

'Nancy Lou'
Double
Tube and sepals pink.
Corolla pure white.
Foliage medium green.
Upright
Bush to 16 cm (6½ in) pot, standard or summer bedder.

'Nicola Jane'
Double
Tube pinkish-cerise.
Sepals cerise.
Corolla pale pink with darker veining.
Foliage medium green.
Garden hardy or summer bedder.

'Norman Mitchinson'
Single
Tube pinkish-white.
Sepals white.
Corolla rich purple.
Foliage medium green.
Upright
Bush to 16 cm (6½ in) pot, standard or summer bedder.

'Northway'
Single
Tube and sepals pale pink.
Corolla cherry red.
Foliage medium to pale green.
Upright

Bush to 12.5 cm (5 in) pot, standard or summer bedder.

'Orange Mirage'
Single
Tube and sepals salmon pink.
Corolla dull orange salmon.
Foliage light green.
Trailer
Basket, half basket or hanging pot.

'Oriental Lace'
Single
Tube and sepals soft light red.
Corolla deep purple.
Foliage small, dark green.
Upright
Small bush to 11 cm ($4\frac{1}{2}$ in) pot, quarter standard or summer bedder.

'Other Fellow'
Single
Tube white.
Sepals white with green tips.
Corolla pink with white shading at the base.
Foliage small, medium green.
Upright
Bush to 16 cm ($6\frac{1}{2}$ in) pot, standard and summer bedder.

'Our Ted'
Triphylla
Tube, sepals and corolla white with a faint pink flush.
Foliage medium green.
Upright
Triphylla classes.

'Pacquesa'
Single to semi-double
Tube and sepals deep red.
Corolla white with red veins.
Foliage parsley green.
Upright
Bush to 16 cm ($6\frac{1}{2}$ in) pot, standard or summer bedder.

'Papoose'
Single
Tube and sepals scarlet.
Corolla dark purple.
Foliage small, medium green.
Lax upright.
Small bush to 11 cm ($4\frac{1}{2}$ in) pot, quarter standard, summer bedder.

'Party Frock'
Semi-double
Tube and sepals rose pink.
Corolla pastel blue, splashed and veined rose pink.
Foliage medium green with reddish veins.
Upright
Bush to 16 cm ($6\frac{1}{2}$ in) pot, standard and summer bedder.

'Patricia Ewart'
Single
Tube and sepals crimson.
Corolla rhodamine pink.
Foliage medium green.
Upright
Bush to 16 cm ($6\frac{1}{2}$ in) pot, standard, summer bedder. Hardy in sheltered areas.

'Paul Roe'
Double
Tube and sepals crimson.
Corolla violet with crimson veins.
Foliage light green.
Upright
Bush to 12.5 cm (5 in) pot, quarter standard or summer bedder.

'Paula Jane'
Semi-double
Tube venetian pink.
Sepals carmine rose.
Corolla beetroot purple changing to ruby red.
Foliage medium green, reddish stems.
Upright
Bush to 16 cm ($6\frac{1}{2}$ in) pot, quarter standard or summer bedder.

'Pearl Farmer'
Single
Tube and sepals carmine.
Corolla amethyst violet with carmine veining, saucer-shaped.
Foliage medium green.
Upright
Bush to 16 cm ($6\frac{1}{2}$ in) pot, standard or summer bedder.

'Pennine'
Single
Tube carmine.
Sepals white.
Corolla dark violet blue.
Foliage medium green.
Upright
Bush to 16 cm ($6\frac{1}{2}$ in) pot, half standard or summer bedder.

'Peppermint Stick'
Double
Tube carmine rose.
Sepals carmine.
Corolla royal purple in the centre, outer petals splashed pink.
Foliage medium to darkish green.
Upright
Bush to 16 cm ($6\frac{1}{2}$ in) pot, quarter standard or summer bedder.

'Perky Pink'
Double
Tube pale pink.
Sepals pink with green tips.
Corolla white, flushed pale pink and with pink veins.
Foliage medium green.
Upright
Bush to 16 cm ($6\frac{1}{2}$ in) pot or summer bedder.

'Perry Park'
Single
Tube and sepals pale pink.
Corolla bright rose pink.
Foliage medium green.
Upright
Bush to 16 cm ($6\frac{1}{2}$ in) pot, standard or summer bedder.

'Petronella'
Double
Tube and sepals flesh pink.
Corolla pale lavender.
Foliage medium green.
Upright
Standard or summer bedder.

'Phyllis'
Single to semi-double
Tube and sepals rose red.
Corolla deeper shade of rose red.
Foliage medium green.
Upright
Standard, pyramid, pillar, fan, espalier, summer bedder.

'Pinch Me'
Double
Tube white.
Sepals white with green tips.
Corolla bishop's purple, pink at the base.
Foliage medium green.
Trailer
Half basket, hanging pot or summer bedder.

'Pink Bon Accorde'
Single
Tube and sepals pale pink.
Corolla pale rose pink.
Foliage medium green.
Upright
Bush to 16 cm ($6\frac{1}{2}$ in) pot, quarter standard or summer bedder.

'Pink Darling'
Single
Tube dark pink.
Sepals pale pink.
Corolla pinkish-lilac.
Foliage medium green.
Upright
Bush to 11 cm ($4\frac{1}{2}$ in) pot or quarter standard.

'Pink Fairy'
Double
Tube and sepals pink.
Corolla pink with darker veining.
Foliage medium green.
Upright
Bush to 16 cm ($6\frac{1}{2}$ in) pot or quarter standard.

'Pink Galore'
Double
Tube pink.
Sepals pink with green tips.
Corolla soft rose pink.
Foliage dark glossy green.
Trailer
Basket, half basket or hanging pot.

'Pink Marshmallow'
Double
Tube and sepals pale pink.
Corolla white with pink veining.

Foliage light green.
Trailer
Basket, half basket or hanging pot.

'Pink Pearl'
Double
Tube and sepals pale pink.
Corolla deep rose pink.
Foliage medium green.
Upright
Bush to 16 cm ($6\frac{1}{2}$ in) pot, standard, fan, espalier, pillar, pyramid or summer bedder.

'Pirbright'
Single
Tube and sepals rhodamine pink.
Corolla cyclamen purple.
Foliage medium green.
Upright
Bush to 12.5 cm (5 in) pot, quarter standard or summer bedder.

'Pixie'
Single
Tube and sepals carmine red.
Corolla mauve purple, veined carmine.
Foliage yellow green with reddish veining.
Upright
Bush or shrub to 16 cm ($6\frac{1}{2}$ in) pot, summer bedder or garden hardy.

'Playford'
Single
Tube and sepals baby pink.
Corolla bluish-mauve, small.
Foliage medium green.
Upright
Bush to 9 cm ($3\frac{1}{2}$ in) pot or quarter standard.

'Plenty'
Single
Tube carmine.
Sepals neyron rose.
Corolla violet purple.
Foliage dark green.
Upright
Bush to 16 cm ($6\frac{1}{2}$ in) pot, quarter standard or summer bedder.

'Pop Whitlock'
Single
Tube and sepals pale pink.
Corolla amethyst violet.
Foliage variegated silvery green with a creamy white edge.
Upright
Ornamental classes to 16 cm ($6\frac{1}{2}$ in) pot, quarter standard or summer bedder.

'Postiljon'
Single
Tube white, flushed pink.
Sepals creamy white, flushed rose pink.
Corolla rosy purple, white at the base.
Foliage small, medium green.
Trailer
Basket, half basket or hanging pot.

'President Margaret Slater'
Single
Tube white.
Sepals white, flushed pink.
Corolla mauve pink, overlaid salmon pink.
Foliage light to medium green.
Trailer
Basket, half basket or hanging pot.

'President Leo Boullemier'
Single
Tube white.
Sepals white, streaked magenta.
Corolla magenta blue ageing to bluish-pink.
Foliage dark green.
Upright
Bush to 16 cm ($6\frac{1}{2}$ in) pot or standard.

'President Stanley Wilson'
Single to semi-double.
Tube carmine.
Sepals carmine with green tips.
Corolla rosy carmine.
Foliage medium green.
Trailer
Basket, half basket or hanging pot.

'Preston Guild'
Single
Tube and sepals white.
Corolla violet, blue grey, small.
Foliage small, medium green.

Upright
Bush to 16 cm (6½ in) pot, standard or summer bedder.

'Prince Syray'
Single
Tube dawn pink.
Sepals deeper shade of pink.
Corolla vermilion with neyron rose shading on the edges of the petals.
Foliage medium green.
Upright
Bush to 16 cm (6½ in) pot or standard.

'Princessita'
Single
Tube and sepals white.
Corolla dark rose pink.
Foliage medium to darkish green.
Trailer
Basket, half basket or hanging pot.

'Prosperity'
Double
Tube and sepals crimson.
Corolla pale neyron rose with rose red veining.
Foliage dark glossy green.
Upright
Bush to 16 cm (6½ in) pot, standard, summer bedder or garden hardy.

'Pumila'
Single
Tube and sepals crimson red.
Corolla purple, very small.
Foliage medium to dark green, small.
Garden hardy, particularly for rockeries.

'R.A.F.'
Tube and sepals red.
Corolla rose pink, veined and splashed cerise.
Foliage medium green.
Lax upright.
Bush to 16 cm (6½ in) pot, hanging pot or summer bedder.

'Ravensbarrow'
Single
Tube and sepals red.
Corolla very dark purple, almost black on opening.
Foliage small, dark green.
Upright
Bush to 12.5 cm (5 in) pot, standard or summer bedder.

'Red Spider'
Single
Tube and sepals crimson.
Corolla rose madder, deeper on the petal edges.
Foliage medium green.
Trailer
Half basket or hanging pot.

'Riccartonii'
Tube and sepals red.
Corolla purple.
Foliage small, medium green.
Upright
Hedging plant to 1.5 m (5 ft) or garden hardy.

'Ridestar'
Double
Tube and sepals scarlet.
Corolla deep lavender blue.
Foliage medium green with reddish veins.
Upright
Bush to 16 cm (6½ in) pot, standard or summer bedder.

'Robbie'
Single
Tube and sepals pale magenta.
Corolla white, small and bell-shaped.
Foliage medium green with red veins.
Upright
Bush or shrub to 12.5 cm (5 in) pot, quarter standard or summer bedder.

'Rolla'
Double
Tube and sepals pale pink.
Corolla pure white with pink tinges at the base.
Foliage light green.
Upright
Bush to 16 cm (6½ in) pot, standard, pyramid or pillar, summer bedder.

'Ron Ewart'
Single
Tube and sepals white.
Corolla rose bengal, white at the base of the petals.
Foliage small, medium green.
Upright
Bush to 12.5 cm (5 in) pot, quarter standard or summer bedder.

'Rose of Castile'
Single
Tube white with a green tinge.
Sepals white, green tips.
Corolla reddish-purple, white at the base and with a white streak in the centre of each petal.
Foliage small, medium green.
Upright
Bush to 16 cm (6½ in) pot, standard, pillar, pyramid or summer bedder.

'Rose of Castile Improved'
Single
Tube and sepals pink.
Corolla reddish-violet with deep pink veins, ageing to reddish-purple
Foliage light to medium green.
Upright
Bush to 16 cm (6½ in) pot, standard, pillar, pyramid or summer bedder.

'Rose of Denmark'
Single
Tube and sepals white.
Corolla rosy purple with rose pink veins.
Foliage medium green
Lax upright.
Bush to 16 cm (6½ in) pot, half basket or hanging pot.

'Rosecroft Beauty'
Single to semi-double.
Tube and sepals crimson.
Corolla white with crimson veining.
Foliage pale green edged cerise and cream, small.
Upright
Bush to 11 cm (4½ in) pot, quarter standard or summer bedder.

'Roy Walker'
Double
Tube and sepals white.
Corolla white.
Foliage medium green.
Upright
Bush to 12.5 cm (5 in) pot, quarter standard or summer bedder.

'Royal Purple'
Single to semi-double.
Tube and sepals cerise.
Corolla purple with red veins.
Foliage medium green.
Upright
Bush to 16 cm (6½ in), standard or summer bedder.

'Royal Velvet'
Double
Tube and sepals crimson.
Corolla deep purple, outer petals splashed with crimson.
Foliage medium green.
Upright
Bush to 16 cm (6½ in) pot, half standard or summer bedder.

'Rufus'
Single
Tube, sepals and corolla bright red.
Foliage medium green.
Upright
Bush to 16 cm (6½ in) pot, standard or summer bedder.

'Sandboy'
Single
Tube pinkish-white.
Sepals very deep pink.
Corolla very dark mauve, small and bell-shaped.
Foliage medium green.
Upright
Bush to 16 cm (6½ in) pot, quarter standard, and will do well in the house.

'Santa Barbara'
Single
Tube and sepals pale pink.
Upright
Bush to 12.5 cm (5 in) pot, quarter standard or summer bedder.

'Saturnus'
Single

Tube and sepals red.
Corolla light purple with reddish veins.
Foliage glossy medium green.
Upright
Bush to 16 cm ($6\frac{1}{2}$ in) pot, summer bedder or garden hardy in sheltered areas.

'Scarcity'
Single
Tube and sepals deep scarlet.
Corolla deep purple.
Foliage medium green.
Upright
Bush to 16 cm ($6\frac{1}{2}$ in) pot, standard or garden hardy.

'Sealand Prince'
Single
Tube and sepals light red.
Corolla pale violet purple.
Foliage light to medium green.
Upright
Garden hardy or summer bedder.

'Sharpitor'
Single
Tube and sepals pale pinkish-white.
Corolla slightly darker than the sepals.
Foliage variegated pale cream and green.
Upright
Garden hardy.

'Siobhan'
Semi-double
Tube rose pink.
Sepals white, flushed pink.
Corolla white, tinged pink at the base.
Foliage medium green.
Upright
Bush or shrub to 16 cm ($6\frac{1}{2}$ in) pot, standard or summer bedder.

'Snowcap'
Semi-double
Tube and sepals scarlet.
Corolla white with reddish veins.
Foliage medium to dark green, small.
Upright
Bush to 16 cm ($6\frac{1}{2}$ in) pot, standard or summer bedder.

'Sonata'
Double
Tube white, tinged green.
Sepals pink with green tips.
Corolla white, veined pink.
Foliage medium green.
Upright
Bush to 16 cm ($6\frac{1}{2}$ in) pot or summer bedder.

'Son of Thumb'
Single to semi-double
Tube and sepals cerise.
Corolla lilac, small.
Foliage small, medium green.
Upright
Bush or shrub to 16 cm ($6\frac{1}{2}$ in) pot, quarter standard, summer bedder or garden hardy.

'Sophisticated Lady'
Double
Tube and sepals pale pink.
Corolla white.
Foliage medium green with reddish veins.
Trailer
Half basket or hanging pot.

'Southgate'
Double
Tube and sepals pale pink.
Corolla soft pink with deeper pink veining.
Foliage medium green.
Upright
Bush to 16 cm ($6\frac{1}{2}$ in) pot, summer bedder or half basket.

'Spion Kop'
Double
Tube and sepals rose red.
Corolla white with rose red veining.
Foliage dull green.
Upright
Bush to 16 cm ($6\frac{1}{2}$ in) pot or summer bedder.

'Stella Ann'
Triphylla
Tube poppy red.

Sepals Chinese coral with green tips.
Corolla Indian orange.
Foliage olive green.
Upright
Triphylla classes or summer bedder.

'Strawberry Delight'
Double
Tube and sepals crimson.
Corolla white, veined pink.
Foliage yellowish-green with a bronzy sheen.
Lax upright.
Ornamental classes or garden hardy.

'Sunray'
Single
Tube red.
Sepals pink.
Corolla purplish-cerise.
Foliage light green with creamy white edges and flushed cerise.
Upright
Ornamental classes or summer bedder.

'Susan Travis'
Single
Tube and sepals pink.
Corolla rose pink.
Foliage dull medium green.
Upright
Garden hardy.

'Swanley Gem'
Single
Tube and sepals scarlet.
Corolla violet with reddish veins, saucer-shaped.
Foliage small, medium green.
Upright
Bush to 16 cm ($6\frac{1}{2}$ in) pot or summer bedder.

'Swingtime'
Double
Tube and sepals scarlet.
Corolla white with scarlet veining.
Foliage medium to darkish green with red veins.
Lax upright.
Basket, half basket or hanging pot.

'Taddle'
Single
Tube and sepals rose pink.
Corolla white, veined pink at the base.
Foliage light green.
Upright
Bush or shrub to 16 cm ($6\frac{1}{2}$ in) pot, standard or summer bedder.

'Taffeta Bow'
Double
Tube pink.
Sepals carmine rose.
Corolla purple violet.
Foliage dark green with crimson veins.
Trailer
Basket, half basket or hanging pot.

'Tennessee Waltz'
Semi-double
Tube and sepals rose madder.
Corolla lilac lavender, splashed with rose pink.
Foliage medium green.
Upright
Bush or shrub to 16 cm ($6\frac{1}{2}$ in) pot, standard or summer bedder.

'Thalia'
Triphylla
Tube and sepals flame red.
Corolla orange scarlet.
Foliage dark olive green with magenta veins.
Upright
Triphylla classes, bush to 16 cm ($6\frac{1}{2}$ in) pot, half standard or summer bedder.

'Ting a ling'
Single
Tube, sepals and corolla white.
Foliage medium green.
Upright
Bush to 16 cm ($6\frac{1}{2}$ in) pot, standard or summer bedder.

'Tom Thumb'
Single to semi-double.
Tube and sepals carmine.
Corolla mauve purple, small.
Foliage small, medium green.
Upright
Bush or shrub to 16 cm ($6\frac{1}{2}$ in) pot, quarter standard, summer bedder or garden hardy.

'Tom West'
Single
Tube and sepals red.
Corolla purple.
Foliage variegated pale greyish-green and cream.
Upright
Ornamental classes or summer bedder.

'Trail Blazer'
Double
Tube and sepals crimson.
Corolla rosy mauve.
Foliage medium green.
Trailer
Half basket or hanging pot.

'Trailing Queen'
Tube and sepals red.
Corolla dark red.
Foliage reddish-bronze.
Trailer
Half basket or hanging pot.

'Trase'
Double
Tube and sepals carmine.
Corolla white, veined cerise.
Foliage small, medium green.
Upright
Garden hardy.

'Traudschen Bonstedt'
Triphylla
Tube and sepals light rose.
Corolla light salmon pink.
Foliage light sage green.
Upright
Triphylla classes or summer bedder.

'Troika'
Semi-double
Tube rose red.
Sepals white.
Corolla light blue, shading to lilac rose.
Foliage medium green.
Lax upright.
Bush to 16 cm ($6\frac{1}{2}$ in) pot, half basket or hanging pot.

'Trumpeter'
Triphylla
Tube, sepals and corolla pale geranium lake.
Foliage bluish-green.
Trailer
Hanging pot or half basket.

'Tsjiep'
Single
Tube and sepals cream.
Corolla blood red, maturing to claret rose, small.
Foliage fuchsia green.
Upright
Bush to 11 cm ($4\frac{1}{2}$ in) pot, quarter standard or summer bedder.

'Unique'
Semi-double
Tube white, tinged pink.
Sepals white.
Corolla rose madder, small.
Foliage light green.
Upright
Bush to 11 cm ($4\frac{1}{2}$ in) pot, quarter standard or summer bedder.

'Upward Look'
Single
Tube and sepals carmine.
Corolla pale roseine purple, held erect.
Foliage dull medium green.
Upright
Bush to 16 cm ($6\frac{1}{2}$ in) pot, standard or summer bedder.

'Vanessa Jackson'
Single
Tube salmon red.
Sepals salmon orange.
Corolla salmon orange, shading to orange red.
Foliage medium green, tinged bronze.
Trailer
Half basket or hanging pot.

'Viva Ireland'
Single
Tube and sepals pale pink.
Corolla lilac blue.
Foliage medium to darkish green.
Lax upright.
Bush to 12.5 cm (5 in) pot or half basket.

'Vivienne Thompson'
Double

Tube and sepals rhodamine pink.
Corolla white, veined neyron rose.
Foliage medium green.
Upright
Bush or shrub to 16 cm ($6\frac{1}{2}$ in) pot or quarter standard.

'Waveney Waltz'
Single
Tube and sepals pale pink.
Corolla white.
Foliage light green.
Upright
Bush to 16 cm ($6\frac{1}{2}$ in) pot, standard or summer bedder.

'Wave of Life'
Single
Tube and sepals scarlet.
Corolla magenta purple.
Foliage greenish-yellow and gold.
Lax bush.
Ornamental classes or summer bedder.

'Wendy Leedham'
Double
Tube and sepals delft rose.
Corolla white, flushed red.
Foliage medium green.
Upright
Bush or shrub to 16 cm ($6\frac{1}{2}$ in) pot, standard or summer bedder.

'White Pixie'
Single
Tube and sepals red.
Corolla white with reddish veins.
Foliage yellowish-green with red veins.
Upright
Bush or shrub to 16 cm ($6\frac{1}{2}$ in) pot, standard, summer bedder or garden hardy.

'Winston Churchill'
Double
Tube and sepals pink.
Corolla lavender blue with pink veins.
Foliage medium green.
Upright
Bush to 16 cm ($6\frac{1}{2}$ in) pot, quarter standard or summer bedder.

'W. P. Wood'
Single
Tube and sepals scarlet.
Corolla purple, small.
Foliage dark green.
Upright
Bush to 12.5 cm (5 in) pot or garden hardy.

Glossary

Anther	The part of the stamens bearing the pollen.
Axil	The angle formed by the junction of leaf and stem, from which new shoots of flowers develop.
Berry	The fleshy fruit containing the seeds; the ovary after fertilization.
Break	To branch or send out new growth from dormant wood.
Calyx	The sepals and tube together; the outer part of the flower.
Corolla	The collective term for the petals; the inner part of the flower.
Cultivar	A cultivated variety, a cross between two hybrids, or a species and a hybrid. Normally written cv.
Double	A flower with eight or more petals.
Fasciation	A condition often found in outdoor fuchsias where two stems and/or flowers appear to be growing into one another. The cause is not known.
Filament	The stalk of the stamen.
Hybrid	A cross between two species.
Node	Part of the stem at which a leaf or bud arises.
Ovary	The part containing the ovules which, after fertilization, swells and encloses the seeds.
Pedicel	The flower stalk.
Petal	A division of the corolla.
Petaloid	Petal-like. Normally used to describe the smaller outer petals of the corolla.
Petiole	The leaf stalk.
Pilose	Having hairs on the surface of leaves or flower parts.
Pinch	To remove the growing tips.
Pistil	The female part of the flower, consisting of the ovary, stigma and style.
Semi-double	A fuchsia with five, six or seven petals.
Sepals	Normally four which, with the tube, form the calyx, the outermost part of the flower.
Sepaloid	Sepal-like.
Single	A fuchsia with four petals only.
Sport	A shoot different in character from the typical growth of the parent plant, often giving rise to a new cultivar. Also known as a mutation.

Stamen	The male part of the flower comprising the filament and anther.
Stop	To remove the growing tips.
Style	The stalk carrying the stigma.
Tube	The elongated part of the calyx, correctly called the hypanthium.
Variety	Botanically a variant of the species, but formerly used to denote what is now correctly called a cultivar.

Recommended Books

The following books, many of which are now out of print and can be obtained only through libraries and second-hand bookshops, are recommended for further reading.

American Fuchsia Society, *Fuchsia Culture*, 1984

American Fuchsia Society, *New A–Z on Fuchsias*, 1976

Beckett, K. A., *Fuchsias*, Aura, 1985

Berry and Raven, *Annals of the Missouri Botanic Garden*, Vol 69/1, 1982

Boullemier, L. B., *Checklist of Species, Hybrids and Cultivars of the Genus Fuchsia*, Blandford Press, 1985

Boullemier, L. B., *Growing and Showing Fuchsias*, David & Charles, 1986

Boullemier, L. B., *Fascinating Fuchsias*, 1973

British Fuchsia Society, *Fuchsia Grower's Handbook*, 1983

Butler, L., *Fuchsias in Australia*, Guyra, 1986

Cesar, J., *Les Fuchsias*, Rustica, 1981

Clapham, S., *Fuchsias for House and Garden*, David & Charles, 1982

Clark, D., *Fuchsias for Greenhouse and Garden*, Collingridge, 1987

Dale, A. D., *An Illustrated Guide to Growing Fuchsias*, Grange, 1986

Dutch Fuchsia Society, *Dutch Checklist and Addenda*, 1977

Essig, E. O., *A Checklist of Fuchsias*, AFS, 1936

Ewart, R., *Fuchsia Lexicon*, Blandford Press, 1982

Ewart, R., *Fuchsia Lexicon*, 2nd edn, Blandford Press, 1987

Fessler, A., *Fuchsien für Haus und Garten*, Kosmos, 1980

Gaucher, M., *Les Fuchsias de l'Ombre et de Lumiere*, Rustique, 1979

Goulding, E. J., *Fuchsias*, Bartholomew, 1973

Jennings, K. and Miller, V., *Growing Fuchsias*, Croom Helm, 1979

Manthey, G., *Fuchsien*, Ulmer, 1983

Munz, P., *A Revision of the Genus Fuchsia*, Californian Academy of Sciences, 1943

Nijhuis, M., *Fuchsias van stek tot stam*, J. H. Gottmer, 1986

NKFV, *Fuchsias hebben en houden*, J. H. Gottmer, 1985

Porcher, F., *Histoire et Culture du Fuchsia*, Libraire Centrale, 1857

Proudley, B. and V., *Fuchsias in Colour*, Blandford Press, 1975

Proudley, B. and V., *How to Grow Fuchsias*, Blandford Press, 1983

Puttock, A. G., *Lovely Fuchsias*, Gifford, 1959

Puttock, A. G., *Pelargoniums and Fuchsias*, Collingridge, 1959

Thorne, T., *Fuchsias for all Purposes*, Collingridge, 1959

Tomlinson, V., *Fuchsias in Southern Africa*, Khenty Press, 1976

Travis, J., *Fuchsia Culture*, 1955

Van der Laan, *Fuchsias het hele jaar door*, Thieme et Cie, 1974

Wells, G., *Fuchsias*, Wisley, 1976
Wilson, S.J. *Fuchsias*, Faber and Faber, 1965
Witham Fogg, H., *Begonias and Fuchsias*, Foyle, 1958
Wood, W. P., *A Fuchsia Survey*, Benn, 1950

General Index

Index of Plants